IN ANCIENT AND LATER POETICS

The Philosophical
Foundations of
Literary Criticism

G. N. Giordano Orsini

Southern Illinois
University Press
Carbondale and Edwardsville

Feffer & Simons, Inc.
London and Amsterdam

Library of Congress Cataloging in Publication Data

Orsini, Gian Napoleone Giordano
  Organic unity in ancient and later poetics.

  Bibliography: p.
  Includes index.
  1. Poetics—History. I. Title.
  PN1035.07   881'.01'09   75-17927
  ISBN 0-8093-0728-6

To my wife,
Margaret Ward Giordano Orsini

Contents

Preface ix

1 Prelude: The Antinomies of Criticism 1

2 The Pre-Socratic Preparation 7

3 Early Literary Criticism 19

4 Plato 30

5 A Cursory Glance at the Scholarship on
  Phaedrus 264C 47

6 Aristotle 63

7 A Parenthetical but Unavoidable Excursus
  into *Mimesis* 67

8 Organic Unity in Aristotle 77

9 Later Criticism 91

Notes 101

Selected Bibliography 111

Index 115

Preface

In this book I have attempted to trace the idea of organic unity in poetry—i.e., the correlation of the parts of a poem to each other and to the whole, with all that follows from that—to its sources in ancient thought and criticism, which sources are not usually considered by the modern critics who speak of organic unity. I have also made some references to its later developments, but this reference is merely incidental and outlined. A complete account would have called for rewriting the whole history of modern criticism.

For generously given advice and information on the ancients I am indebted to Professor Fritz Solmsen, who however is not to be considered responsible for the conclusions that I draw from it.

I wish also to express my gratitude to my doctors and hospital nurses for the new lease of life which has enabled me to finish this book.

Madison, Wisconsin G. N. Giordano Orsini
November 1974

Organic Unity
in Ancient and Later Poetics

1

Prelude: The Antinomies
of Criticism

✒ There is a tendency in some contemporary criticism to
start every question from scratch, as if it had never been
thought of before and there was nothing behind it, no history, no antecedent. This fosters the illusion that the critic's
views on that question are entirely novel and original, and
the critic may proceed breezily on his way without ever, or
hardly ever, turning back to any precedent, except perhaps
to some favored contemporary, and then concluding by
bringing up his own views as the definitive solution to the
question. Since the same attitude may be taken at the same
time by other critics of differing or opposite views, the result
is the babel that can easily be imagined.

Such a situation turns no doubt to the satisfaction of those
critics and those readers who are reluctant to look back ever
into the past. Horrible prospect: laboring at an exact knowledge of what has been thought before us by other people!
This book is written from a point of view which is almost
the exact opposite of that. I believe that knowledge of the
history of ideas is the lifeblood of any critical conception
that aims at saying something valid that is also new. How
can one know if it is new if one ignores the old?

More specifically, I shall be speaking, rather than of the

history of ideas, of the history of concepts and of theories. "Ideas" has become by and large too vague a term to be of use ("one word is too often profaned/for me to profane it," as the poet said of love). The history of ideas is a noble discipline, but in some of its less worthy practitioners the ideas have become a swarm of many-colored balloons floating aimlessly through empty space. Naturally the term "concept," like all words in the language, is also subject to degradation, (e.g., "a new concept in advertising" or "in cosmetics"), but it has not yet become quite as generalized as idea. The latter term can stand for at least two important and well-defined concepts in the history of philosophy, as the Theory of Ideas in Plato, and as a term for the Absolute in Hegel. Since I may have to refer to both those meanings, the term "concept" should avoid confusion with them. To be specific: I use it to mean a general conception, standing for a number of particular things or thoughts. I do not attribute to it a metaphysical status, merely referring to it as something that is in our minds when we think it—loaded as that simple assertion is with problems, into which I do not intend to enter now. A concept can usually be defined, and under it we subsume a number of subordinate notions. The term "subsume" implies that the connection is a rational one: the generalization actually fits the particulars, and the particulars in turn fit into the generalization, which is all as it should be. This is not just a "family resemblance," but a logical relation.

Furthermore, concepts are not just carelessly drifting all over the place but have connections with each other. Firstly, some have logical connections, implying other concepts, some exclude or contradict others and are incompatible with them, some branch out in several directions and form clusters and systems. It is the business of reflective thought to bring out these relations and place the concepts in their proper relations to each other. Reflective thought is technically called philosophy, a discipline of which most practicing literary critics fight shy. For one thing, it implies the labor of understanding a technical language, that being the way in which these relationships are discussed; and also it involves being careful of such distinctions—to give an example which may concern us, between *transcendent* and *transcendental,* the difference between the two amounting to opposition, the former meaning "beyond experience," the other designating the very conditions of experience. (Plato's Ideas are transcendent, Kant's Categories are transcendental.) Like every good thing, technical language can be abused, and I shall avoid resorting to it too frequently in a book addressed mainly to literary students and critics.

Secondly, but of equal importance, concepts have not only a logical value, but also, as we noted already, a history of their own. That is, they have been formulated by certain thinkers, engaged upon certain problems, and holding certain presuppositions, most of which can be determined historically. All these conditions bear upon the meaning and the validity of a concept. If concepts do not float about in a vacuum, neither do they exist as fixed stars in the unchanging empyrean of eternal truth, as some metaphysicians have conceived them. As historical productions they rise above the stream of time, being clear and distinct in themselves, as Descartes required of them.

The purpose of all this is to prepare the reader for the formulation of some basic critical concepts in their positions of affirmation and negation, as antinomies or conflicting propositions. They all have a bearing upon our main subject, organic unity in poetics. (For typographical reasons, their list is printed on the following page.)

For a solution to these antinomies, we turn to the theory of organic unity. In its original form, as put by Plato in the *Phaedrus* (264C), it begins by assuming a division of the work into parts, but then immediately requires a double concordance or harmony: that of the parts 1) with each other and 2) with the whole. This simple statement is pregnant with consequences for theory and for the practice of criticism.

The Antinomies of Criticism[1]

Pro	Con
1. Every poem can be subjected to analysis and be judged.	1. No poem can be analyzed. No poem can be judged.
2. Every poem is divisible into parts.	2. No poem is divisible into parts.
3. The parts of a poem are its words.	3. There are no such things as isolated words.
4. Every poem can be paraphrased in other words.	4. No poem can be paraphased in other words.
5. Every poem connects with other poems.	5. Every poem exists in itself by itself and does not connect with any other poem.
6. Specifically, every poem is a part of the total *opus* of its author, as well as of the national literature to which he belongs, and must be considered in connection with them.	6. Poems being unique individuals are never part of larger units.

For if we develop it fully, it imports a *synthesis* of the parts, the parts of a poem being differently divided and designated according to the character of the poem. They may, or may not, consist of words, phrases, sentences, periods, or lines, or stanzas, or acts and scenes, etc. the minimum division being that in two parts as in Aristotle's Form and Matter.

Eventually, the theory comes to include the principle of the individuality of the work of art, and this brings a solution to the other antinomies: paraphrases are new compositions, and single poems may, or may not connect with other poems by the same author, depending on the individual character and particular physiognomy of each work. A national literature is not a poetic unit but an assemblage of poetic units; and genres, sources, and influences are not aesthetic values but usually belong to what is called the history of culture on one side of the Atlantic, and the history of ideas on the other.

Even this does not exhaust the definition of a poem; other valuable concepts have been developed in the course of history, an essential one being the concept of the lyrical nature of all poetry. As a great critic said, a good poem should "reflect the colors, the light and shade, the body and soul of the work." This calls for a special sensibility in the critic, which cannot be replaced by general theories however sound.

But we have seen that concepts not only have a logical structure but an historical genesis. This for organic unity has already been shown in Plato, and more will come. The historical place of the antinomies is that the Pros may be said to represent, roughly and incompletely, the trend that is often called the historical school of literary criticism; and the Cons reflect, also roughly and incompletely, what has been called the New Criticism.[2] The rest of this book will follow the development of the organic unity in antiquity, and in a concluding chapter we shall glance rapidly at its later history.

The practical applications of the theory are innumerable. Take Greek tragedy to begin with. Do Greek tragedies possess organic unity? Or does its theatrical structure interfere with it? Do the choruses connect fittingly with the dialogue and the action? Since most Greek tragedies are works of art, the case may be different with each of them. One drastic answer to these questions was that the poetry is to be found principally in the choral songs, the dialogue being definitely inferior; but that has not gained general acceptance. Is the *Divine Comedy* an organic unity? Or, again, does the structure—theological and/or narrative— interrupt the poetry of the dramatic episodes? Are the two parts of Goethe's *Faust* organically united? Or does the first part alone lack that unity? Coming to the moderns, the question is or can be raised continually. Is Joyce's *Ulysses* organic? Or is it merely a miscellany of styles, as an Italian critic called it (*un campionario di stili*)? I can find more unity in Lowry's *Under the Volcano*. Many, if not most, modern poems are very loose in arrangement, and call for subtle perception to see the unity.

And here is an example showing how organic unity can be found in a work belonging to another art, architecture. After enumerating the "elements" of the building—in this case, the church of Santa Maria Novella in Florence—the critic goes on to say: "The architectural 'meaning' of Santa Maria Novella evidently cannot be found in any of these elements (its façade, its arches, its doors, its windows) taken singly, but the spirit and the significance of the work speaks out clearly in the arrangement of its parts. The formal relations among what seem to be jarring elements of three different styles, Romanesque, Gothic, and classical, produce Alberti's unmistakable kind of unity. His façade is a 'harmony,' achieving what Philolaos (fl. 470 B.C.) defined 'the unification of the composed manifold and the accordance of the discordant'."[3] Keeping all this in mind, let us now proceed to the history of the theory.

2

The Pre-Socratic
Preparation

The earliest performances of the Greeks in the field of
literary criticism are largely subject to conjecture. There
are no fully developed critical writings extant before the
age of Socrates, who of course did not himself write, and
very little to go by anyway. Some interferences as to literary
opinion may be made from poems, and a little more from
the fragments of the early philosophers.[1]

From this material we gather that certain fundamental
issues had already been joined. For instance, the issue between didacticism (or moralism) and pure hedonism, or
between the principle that poetry must teach, particularly
teach morality, and the principle that poetry teaches nothing and exists only for pleasure. So, it seems, had the issue
between a rudimental form of realism—i.e., that poetry
consists in the portrayal or reproduction of real things and
people—and "idealism," or the view that poetry is more
than the reproduction of reality—how exactly "more," receives from the beginning different answers. Even more
substantial was the issue between the so-called inspiration
theory, which asserts that poetry is not under the control of
the poet but is vouchsafed to him from a higher source, and
what is really its opposite, the theory that poetry consists of

7

conscious craftsmanship, the rules of which may be formulated, learnt, and taught (and even enforced), but always
under the control of the artist. Sooner or later these discussions bring up the concept of poetic unity, which implies
the concept of unity in the abstract or unity in general, and
the philosophers were already getting concerned with unity
in general.

In the earliest Greek philosophers that we hear of, the
so-called Milesians, the idea of unity appears in the shape
of material unity, or the search for the one substance of
which the world is ultimately composed. Thales is said to
have believed it was water, Anaximenes that it was air, and
Anaximander (who seems to have been the most philosophical of the three) something indeterminate that he called
the *ápeiron* or the unlimited.[2] None of the Milesians appears to have conceived of unity at the most general level,
unity in the abstract, unity in itself, until later thinkers
marked it off by opposing it to Multiplicity as the One and
the Many.

Now this question of the One and the Many constitutes
one of the greatest problems of Greek philosophy,[3] and
perhaps of all philosophy. Some idea of this may be gathered
from the pronouncements of two great writers of a much
later age, one of whom was an historian and the other a
famous essayist. Their statements will serve as a kind of
literary introduction to this famous philosophical question,
which was also implied in the antinomies of the first chapter.
The first quotation is from Edward Gibbon: "The genius
of Plato, informed by his own meditation, or by the traditional knowledge of the priests of Egypt, had ventured to
explore the mysterious nature of the Deity. When he had
elevated his mind to the sublime contemplation of the first,
self-existent, necessary cause of the universe, the Athenian
sage was incapable of conceiving *how* the simple unity of his
essence could admit the infinite variety of distinct and successive ideas which compose the model of the intellectual
world."[4]

Disregarding the dubious reference to the "traditional knowledge of the priests of Egypt," the problem of unity and multiplicity is here stated with reference to theology, in which Gibbon had little faith. But this is how Emerson, the transcendentalist, put it:

"Philosophy is the account which the human mind gives to itself of the constitution of the world. Two cardinal facts lie forever at its base: the one, and the two—Unity, or identity, and 2. Variety. We unite all things by perceiving the law which pervades them; by perceiving the superficial differences and the profound resemblances. But every mental act—this very perception of identity or oneness, recognizes the differences of things. It is impossible to think or to speak without embracing both.

". . . Urged by . . . necessity, the mind returns from the one to that which is not one, but other or many; from the cause to the effect; and affirms the necessary existence of variety, the self-existence of both, as each is involved in the other. These strictly blended elements it is the problem of thought to separate and to reconcile.

". . . These two principles reappear, and interpenetrate all things, all thought; the one, the many."[5]

And later a very different American thinker, William James, had this to say about "the One and the Many": "the most central of all philosophic problems, most central because so pregnant."[6]

We begin with the opposition of the One to the Many. But after a while we begin to see that they are not opposed in every way. Is not every single unit composed of several parts? And, going back into poetics, is not even the shortest poem, say a haiku, composed of a number of lines, and the shortest line composed of a number of words?—even the legendary anonymous French sonnet made up of one-syllable lines: "Fort Belle Elle Dort, Sort Frèle Quelle Mort. / Rose Close La Bise L'a Prise."

Now in a multiplicity the many may be unified by a third factor, an "additional element," as Cornford defines it,[7] which it would be useful to bring out and determine, especially in the case of a poem, since it gives us the key to its poetic value. The total effect produced by this unified multiplicity can be also described as "unity in variety," and has often been so described. "We now approach," as Bosanquet said, "the consideration of the true aesthetic principle recognised by Hellenic antiquity in general. This may be described as the principle that beauty consists in the imaginative or sensuous expression of unity in variety."[8] Even disregarding such terms as "imaginative" and "expression," which were developed by later criticism, it does not seem possible to give the name of the critic who first defined beauty in that way, nor does Bosanquet tell us. But this definition leads to, or implies, the idea that beauty consists in the relationship of parts to a whole, thus introducing the important concept of "the whole," that which confers unity to its parts. The character of this relationship of the parts has been described by various terms, such as "order" (*táxis, kósmos*), "measure" (*métron*), "symmetry" (*symmétria*) and "harmony" (*harmoniá*). With the latter we reach one of the basic ideas of the next Greek philosophical school that we meet in our narrative, the Pythagoreans. Of this school, whose earliest formulations are still somewhat shadowy, it may perhaps be affirmed that they are the first philosophers on record to conceive of the world as made up of pairs of opposites, of which they also courageously made a full list.

This list begins with a pair called "the limit and the unlimited," and proceeds with the following: "odd and even, one and many, right and left, male and female, rest and motion, straight and crooked, light and dark, good and bad, square and oblong"—ten pairs, as given later by Aristotle *Metaphysics* 986A22. In this list, which includes our old friends the One and the Many, it should be noted that the first term is the positive, as in "good and bad," and the second is negative. Taking this into account, we cannot help observing that not all pairs are opposites, such that one excludes the other as "good and bad, one and many." Some pairs we would rather regard as complementary, such that one requires the other, like "male and female." Some pairs in this mixed bag do not seem to be either opposite or complementary, but merely different, such as "square and oblong."

Such an analysis of the mixed bag belongs to later thought. The distinction between opposites and complementaries in that list is to be found in the second century Skeptical philosopher Sextus Empiricus. Sextus also recognized a third class of pairs in the list, and defined it in a way that need not concern us here.[9] This analysis by Sextus was quoted by Hegel in his lectures on the history of philosophy.[10] Yes! Sextus, the arch-Skeptic, is quoted by Hegel, reputedly an arch-dogmatist.

To say simply "the one and the many," without defining it further, does not take us very far in poetics, especially as the Pythagoreans did not proceed to consider poetry, much less to attempt to define poetic unity. But their achievements in other fields of aesthetics were outstanding and must be mentioned here, even if only mentioned. It was to the theory of music that they made their most important contributions, which will be found detailed in histories of ancient thought and of aesthetics.[11] The Pythagoreans appear to have seen cosmic significance to music, and considered the universe as ultimately a kind of harmony.[12] In the words of the poet, they believed that "From harmony, from heavenly harmony / This universal frame began." And they were the first to hear the music of the spheres.

What they actually meant by that I shall not venture to inquire here, but I will pass on to another dyad on the list, possibly more relevant to poetics: viz., the odd-sounding pair, the Limited and the Unlimited ($\pi\acute{\epsilon}\rho\alpha\varsigma$ $\kappa\alpha\grave{\iota}$ $\ddot{\alpha}\pi\epsilon\iota\rho\sigma\nu$). Without going into all the interpretations that have been offered of the pair, it may be mentioned that the Unlimited has been connected with Anaximander's Boundless, the Pythagoreans having provided it with its opposite, the Limit.

The first item in each pair of opposites, as we saw, was

considered the positive one, and the second negative. We can also see that "stability" in certain cases can be preferred to "motion," but "male and female," in that order, is obviously an early example of male chauvinism. In the pairs "odd and even, square and oblong, right and left," the preference for the first in each pair seems curious, but perhaps finds support in the famous Pythagorean theory of numbers or some other belief.

It seems hard to see why Limit should be preferable to Unlimited; yet we are definitely told by Aristotle that for the Pythagoreans evil is of the class of the infinite, and good of the finite.[13] For us moderns, a limit is a boundary, and a restriction, seen unfavorable as a curb to our unlimited freedom of action. The Boundless instead suggests the infinite expanse of unrestricted space and potentiality, for which we moderns have a preference. But we come after the Romantic revolution, which had a decided preference for the Infinite and the unrestricted, even for the vague and indefinite. The Greeks instead, as we see them, had a decided preference, which has been considered a factor of their greatness in art and in thought, for the well defined, the clearly bounded and limited, and hence the shapely and well formed.[14] That is why the limit is considered the positive element. The necessity for both terms may have been conceived something like this: a pattern of the universe cannot be built out of an indeterminate and indefinite substance with no particular qualities; there must be something else, a factor that makes for definition and precision of shape, marking each thing off from the other and assigning it its proper configuration. And that would be the Limit.

See how fruitful this conception is. On one side, we have the vast, indeterminate, nondescript stuff out of which everything is made; but on the other side, we have the Limit, i.e., definiteness of shape and size, and eventually even of configuration and structure. Bring them together, and the whole ordered universe of things and beings comes into view, each thing marked out within its boundaries, and provided with its specific qualities.

And so we may also see why modern historians of thought have discerned in that odd pair, the Limit and the Unlimited, the forerunner of that long-familiar Aristotelian pair, Form and Matter. As long ago as 1909 Otto Gilbert argued that Aristotle, interpreting previous doctrines in the light of his own, had equated the Pythagorean limit and unlimited to his own form and matter.[15] Nestle in his revision of Zeller's summary said of the Pythagoreans: "the cosmic dualism of matter and form, or as they expressed it, of the limited and unlimited."[16] L. L. Whyte in 1951: "The conception of form as the characteristic principle of the thing begins to appear, correlative to the conception of matter. The limit gives form to the unlimited."[17]

If so, the aesthetic relevance of the dyad becomes apparent. For Form and Matter are the most general terms for what in criticism are the Form and Content of a work.[18] And what distinction is more widely and commonly used, and more fundamental in poetics and literary criticism, even though their meaning may receive somewhat different connotations each time? Throughout criticism we find works praised for their form, and censured for their content, or vice versa, or with praise and censure distributed in various proportions between the two. The two terms are indispensable to the most elementary account of a work and may aquire more subtle meanings in the most sophisticated criticism: e.g., the form of *Paradise Lost* is blank verse, and the content is the story of Adam's fall; or, more specifically, the form is that of the Renaissance epic, and the content is the biblical account of original sin. And so forth, through several variations of the reference of the dyad: to language, to style, to imagery, to meter, to structure, and all the interpretations of such things. Whole schools of criticism have been designated by the fact that they lay more stress upon the one than upon the other, and been classified as

Formalists if they consider Form the distinguishing feature of creation, and Content secondary or indifferent.

What if the critic makes content supreme, and judges works by the significance and value, orthodoxy or social relevance, of their content or subject, and considers form secondary or indifferent? This is not an unusual procedure, and is well represented in the history of criticism, but in English we do not have a term to designate it, as we have Formalism for its opposite. Feeling this need, I ventured to suggest Contentualism, a word suggested by Croce's "contenutismo" (I cannot say if coined by him) and given a more English shape. For instance, the attitude of the early critics of Homer (to be discussed in the next section) may be described as generally contentualistic, since it refers almost exclusively to the subject-matter of the Homeric poems, and they had little or nothing to say about their form.

This will take us to the final point in this discussion: how does the dyad, Form and Content, affect the unity of a poem? Is a poem a single indivisible unit, or is it made up of two (or more) factors, and do we have to give up unity? Experience shows that this is not the case. Form and Content are seen by critics to constitute a solid unity, one factor being meaningless without the other.[19] The schools of criticism that make a sharp division between them end up in fallacy. We shall now see how this conception of unity was first formulated, and how it developed and grew, bringing up further consequences and further territories for criticism.

Heraclitus

The next philosopher that we will take notice of is one of the most daring, paradoxical and thought-provoking writers in history. Heraclitus, known as "the obscure" because of the cryptic character of his sayings, wrote a book in prose *On Nature* of which Aristotle[20] quoted the exordium for the purpose of pointing out an ambiguity in it.[21] Even in fragments, which is all that we possess of it, it contains flashes of splendid paradox and splendid insight. Indeed, some of his most startling propositions turn out on examination to be plain common sense. Take his most famous saying, which points to something so simple that a child can understand it, i.e., running water; but the consequences drawn from it are startling—"We cannot step into the same river twice" (fg. 91). Of course not, for the waters of the river are flowing as we step into them, and the river is not the same when we step into it again. Furthermore, we cannot step into the same river even *once* (fg. 49A) for the same reason.[22] This thought was crystallised (probably later) into the formula "everything flows" (πάντα ῥεῖ). But if there is nothing stable in the universe, then it follows that there is nothing that we can fix down in a settled concept and define once for all. The consequences for philosophical thought as well as for ordinary thought seem to be shattering.

For in this way Heraclitus at one stroke cut down all dogmatic, one-sided, one-colored conceptions of the world. Nature changes and man changes, and there is no end to the process. He also said "the way up is the same as the way down" (fg. 60). Absurd? No, common sense: the incline is the same. The moral of it all seems to be that we should avoid the cut-and-dried commonplaces of ordinary thinking, and look for concepts so flexible that they can follow reality in its perpetual movement. Where can we find such concepts?

Heraclitus at first seems to speak only in parables, with striking similes and vivid illustrations, but apparently with no definite formulation of positive doctrine. The great constructive system-builders that followed him, Plato and Aristotle, settled for such concepts as the eternal Ideas and the immutable Essences: but they both will have to cope with Heraclitus and the flux of unremitting change; and they both will do so, each in his own way.

Now if we look at a poem from this point of view of perpetual change, the poem (something which Heraclitus apparently never considered in the abstract) ceases to be a solid object, fixed on the written or printed page, and endowed with specific features and definite qualities. A poem becomes something like Heraclitus' strung bow, that Guthrie so aptly expounds: "Look at a strung bow lying on the ground or leaning against a wall. No movement is visible. To the eyes it appears as a static object, completely at rest. But in fact a continuous tug of war is going on within it, as will become evident if the string is not strong enough or is allowed to perish."[23]

Since this process is a struggle, which may result in victory or in defeat, in a successful poem or in a poor poem, there may be a slowing down or breaking up of the tension, and the work may be botched by the intrusion of some extraneous element, or a deviation into some blind alley.

The fundamental question is how can we adopt a method of thinking that follows reality in its eternal flux and avoid rigidity? Heraclitus's answer lies in the doctrine of the opposites. For Heraclitus the opposite elements of which the world is made up—such as the pairs of opposites listed by the Pythagoreans—are not in static juxtaposition but engaged in eternal warfare with each other, and "war is the father of all" (fg. 53). Life is always fighting death, and wakefulness is always fighting sleep: these examples are Heraclitus's own. And this is what has been called "polarity," taking its name from the opposing poles which are both part of the magnet.[24] Polarity, says the dictionary, is the "manifestation of two opposing attributes, tendencies or principles."[25]

The next step is momentous: this opposition ultimately is harmony, or difference in agreement (fg. 51). A third concept is so postulated, in which the opposites are subsumed and reconciled. So Heraclitus's basic concept of Becoming arises out of the conflict of Being with Not-being, for something which is, and is not at the same time, is obviously in the process of becoming.

This paves the way for what in modern times is called

"dialectic," and has turned out to be one of the most powerful engines for philosophical combat. In its most mature modern form, dialectics was practiced extensively—too extensively—by Hegel, while in the hands of Marx it became the weapon for social revolution, as "dialectical materialism." But Hegel used it to build up one of the most elaborate systems of aesthetics—even if it had been applied to poetry long before in the pseudo Aristotelian *De mundo*:

"Nature too struggles through the contraries and obtains a concord through them, and not through the similar: e.g., she pairs male with female, and establishes its first union through contraries, not through similiars. Art, too, seems to do this, imitating nature: painting mixes on the canvas the elements of the colors white and black, yellow and red, and obtains thus agreement with its model; music mixes high and low notes, long and short, and from different sounds obtains a single harmony. The art of writing blends vowels and consonants and obtains this complete effect. The same results from the words of the obscure Heraclitus: 'connections of the all with the non-all, similar and different, harmony and disharmony, and from all the one, and from one, all.' "[26]

This remarkable passage shows how a doctrine of art can be worked out from the sayings of Heraclitus, even if he himself apparently did not do so. What he had to say about poets was mainly a criticism of the poems of Homer and of Hesiod from what we have called a contentualistic point of view, viz. rejection of the mythology contained in them.

Finally, if there ever is a "finally" with this thinker, we find in Heraclitus a still more postive foundation for constructive thought in his concept of Reason, or the Logos, if that is the correct interpretation. Apparently Heraclitus recognized a positive concept beyond all opposites: the idea of universal Law. He said (fg. 2) "we must follow what is common to all [or, the universal]: but although the Law [*Logos*] is universal, the majority of men live as if they had a private understanding." This apparently is the first de-

nunciation on record of what is rejected as "private thinking," or every man making up his own logic regardless of
reason, society, and history. And it comes from the philosopher of eternal flux—but also of eternal law. There are
indeed hints in Heraclitus of a more profound philosophy
beyond the flux of change, a philosophy of which we can
only catch glimpses. The most detailed and persuasive re-
sonstruction of this philosophy will be found in Guthrie
(1:419–73), and there we must leave it, for it does not seem
to bear directly on aesthetic issues.

3

Early Literary
Criticism

✐ The first notions of poetics, rhetoric, and art criticism appear now, in the fifth century or so, together with the upward thrust of Greek philosophy, which is entering its greatest period. The Eleatic school, as it is now called, may be considered to have the first real metaphysicians Parmenides and Zeno who affirmed the absolute unity of Being and denied the reality of the Many: "Being . . . never was, nor will be, because it is *now,* a whole, altogether, one, uninterrupted."[1] "Nor is being divisible since it is all alike."[2] Since being is indivisible, there is no discussion about the parts of anything and their relation to the whole. Parmenides obviously rejects Heraclitus's views on dialectical becoming, nor did he have anything to say about poetic unity. On the fringes of the Eleatics, Xenophanes appears to be the most explicit in his discussion of poets, for he roundly condemned Homer and Hesiod for their anthropomorphic representation of the gods. He thus continues and stresses the contentualistic criticism of poetry which we have already seen in Heraclitus. Among other tendencies in philosophy, Empedocles is a striking figure whose fate or legend has been of inspiration to later poets, but does not seem to have written on the subject of poetry itself.

Democritus alone is stated to have written on critical problems; unfortunately, his books on the subject are all lost. But the titles remain, and they are suggestive: *On Rhythms and Harmony, On Poetry, On the Beauty of Words, On Well- and Ill-sounding Letters, On Homer,* and *On Singing*—a whole library of literary criticism, and a lot obviously not on content but on formal elements. One fragment of his roundly asserts the divine inspiration of poets.[3]

But these early philosophers wrote on problems concerning the other arts. Tatarkiewicz, who gives a full exposition of what is known in this regard, summarizes the situation thus: "Empedocles as well as Xenophanes concerned himself with primary colors, and like Democrititus, Anaxogoras and Agatharcus studies deformations caused by perspective" (1:111). He also notes the beginning of relativistic theories of taste in Xenophanes and the *Dialéxesis* (or *Dissoi Lógoi*) (1:105–6, 111).

Toward the second half of the fifth century the artists themselves began to write books on their art. We hear that Apelles wrote a book on painting, and that Protogenes wrote two. Polykleitos is considered to have been a great theoretician and to have enhanced the prestige of artists by showing that they could theorize as well. Catchwords and slogans like "symmetry" and "grace" (*cháris*) begin to circulate, which are capable of being extended to poetry. The aesthetic ideas that we have seen germinating at the time of the Pythagoreans and of Heraclitus now undergo a further development which brings them nearer to the theories we are aiming at, namely the definition of beauty as unity in variety.

All this train of reasoning, and this definition, must be left without the name of an author, but it seems to have been made some time in the fifth century B.C. The first name of a thinker we meet in this connection is that of the late Pythagorean, Philolaos (latter half of the fifth century), to whom is attributed (doubtfully) the following definition: "Harmony is the unity of many mixed (elements), and an agreement between the disagreeing." We shall see more about the development of this doctrine in ancient times.

The first quotation of "Philolaos" is from K. Freeman's *Ancilla,* page 75. For the doubts cast on the authenticity of the fragments of Philolaos, see Guthrie, 1:330–33. Whoever wrote that definition was an ancient Greek, and that definition as we saw was found useful by a contemporary critic of an architectural masterpiece, which confirms its aesthetic value. In the last analysis, Croce's pronouncement on it is as follows: " 'unity' and 'unity in variety' are resolved into generalized determinations of art as a spiritual activity."[4]

I will now introduce what may be called the hero of this narrative, the principle of organic unity. Its first appearance in extant literature is perfectly clear and definite: it was formulated explicitly for the first time by Plato in the *Phaedrus* (264B), in a passage which will be analyzed in detail in the following section. But Plato's definition of this unity is so simple and so lucid that it may be quoted at once: it consists in the agreement of the parts of a work with each other and with the whole. This, as we shall see, has many implications and consequences.

I wish to introduce next what may be called the villain of this narrative, which is the principle of disunity, of analysis without synthesis, of systematic division and subdvision, which in logic produces the so-called Tree of Porphyry and in poetics the doctrine of literary genres. This method of classification and subordination, and of juxtaposition instead of conjunction, may be summed up in one antithesis, that of the mechanical against the organic. In history the mechanical may be said to follow the organic almost as its shadow. Follow? Sometimes it precedes. And if organic unity can be traced to Plato, so can the other principle.[5] To avoid prejudice, I suppose to call it by a neutral term devoid of negative associations: Taxonomy.

Taxonomy takes place every time we divide a whole into parts, and then omit to look for the principle of unity that binds them together and makes them into a whole. It occurs

in all the distinctions of poems into parts that we have
been enumerating, into words, lines, stanzas, acts, episodes,
chapters, etc., and so on to the more sophisticated dissec-
tions in rhetoric and in modern poetics. It is unquestionably
a useful and even necessary procedure in the early stages
of literary discussion. A new work is puzzling by its very
newness, and we may have to take it apart to grasp its details; even in later stages of the discussion we may have to
refer backward and forward to various points in the poem.
But as a system of critical interpretation it tends to lead us
away from consideration of the whole. And defining the
whole is apt to be more difficult than separating the parts;
but then defining the whole is the proper task of true
literary judgment, while taxonomy is the procedure of much
"analytical criticism" and possibly even of "structuralism."
As Edward Caird put it:

"The abstracting or *analytic* process, by which unity is
separated *from* difference, is nothing without the *synthetic*
process, by which unity is discerned in difference, as the
principle which at once originates and overcomes it. The
true method, therefore, is a method which combines analysis and synthesis in one, and which moves forwards by a
perpetual *systole-dyastole*, at once towards a higher unity
of thought and towards a more complete determination and
articulation of all the facts embraced under it. . . . its aim is
to make knowledge . . . an *organic* system, in which every
part is seen in its due relation to the other parts, because it
is seen to be determined by the one principle which gives
life to the whole."[6]

Croce relegated it to the domain of the practical (not the
theoretical, as the aesthetic is) and to the utilitarian (not to
the ethical). Yet, as Croce said, this method "was useful,
necessary, and irreplaceable: through it the infinite manifes-
tations of reality are ordered in genres and species and sub-
species, and connections and laws are established among
these *schemata,* so that it is possible to rise from them to the
individual facts and grasp them intuitively in their his-

torical individuality. One cannot even imagine the disaster, the world-cataclysm that would ensue if this classificatory function were denied to the human mind."[7] Of its main application to literary criticism, the theory of literary genres, Goethe said: "this compartmented cupboard, by means of which the inner concept of poetry is destroyed."[8] Having introduced the main characters of my story, I will now proceed with the narrative itself.

From the fifth century B.C. to the third century B.C. Greek philosophy follows an almost continuous course of development that goes from the Sophists to Socrates, from Socrates to Plato, and from Plato to Aristotle. All of these thinkers had something to say on poetry, and the last two had a lot to say, much of it bearing on the concept of poetic unity. But this development was not of course smooth and uniform or without turns and complications, which we shall observe as they come up.

First, the Sophists. By this time, it should be unnecessary to repeat the well-know fact that the name Sophist did not originally bear the discreditable denotation is acquired after Plato, who is largely responsible for it. By modern historians the Sophists are described as itinerant teachers of speech and the art of debating, who taught these arts for a fee. In this they differed from the earlier Greek thinkers, who behaved like sages or prophets, only too glad to impart their teachings to anybody freely and without compensation. So what the Sophists had mainly in common was their professional attitude, coupled with the fact that some of their earnings were enormous, for they operated in an age when every citizen, particularly every Athenian, was eager to floor his fellow citizen in open debate either political or forensic. The pecuniary consideration, and the consequent big profits, no doubt contributed to their ill fame.[9] But even in the powerful writings of the man who contributed most to their discredit, Plato (with the help of Xenophon), one gathers that they had things to teach that were of consequence for philosophy and for criticism.

Although they did not possess a common doctrine, they have been credited with initiating an important turn in Greek thought—from speculations on the universe to investigations about man, from nature to mind, in one word, from the objective to the subjective. So here we come upon that famous pair (object and subject) that Carlyle heard so often recurring, as he vividly describes, in Coleridge's conversation: "I still recollect his 'object' and 'subject,' terms of continual reference in the Kantian province, and how he sung and sniffled them into 'om-m-mject' and 'sum-m-mject,' with a kind of solemn quake or quiver, as he rolled along. No talk, in this century or in any other, could be more surprising."[10]

But the reader need not be afraid of them. They will not bite, and here they are used only to refer to the Sophists' shift in interest from, say, the external to the internal, from the universe to man, from nature to mind. In any acceptance, objective and subjective are opposites, and what comes under the one does not come under the other. A purely subjective feeling is not an objective reality, and vice versa. Yet these two opposites are correlative. They necessarily refer to each other; the object is what stands in front of a subject, and the subject becomes such because an object is presented to it. It may also be put thus: a thought requires a thinker, and a thinker requires a thought, but one is not the other.

Be that as it may, the Sophists' interest in argument led them to study ways of presenting things and to techniques for producing an effect, in short, to ways of composing a fine speech, and "fine" implies some degree of aesthetic evaluation. So some of the investigations of the Sophists were more or less concerned with the beautiful in art.

We begin to hear more of literary criticism. At first it was concerned mainly with the poems of Homer, the most important poetry to date, as in the Glaucon and other mentioned by Plato in the *Ion* (530D); Glaucon is also referred to by Aristotle (*Poetics* 1461B1). But the drama now reaches its climax, and we hear of critics of tragedy, like another Glaucon mentioned by Aristotle (*Rhetoric* 1403B26). However, we do not have a scrap of their writings. Grammatical analysis, an indispensable subsidiary to exegesis, also begins, and we hear that the great Sophist Protagoras made important contributions to it.[11] It is if course part of the analysis of speech, which interested the Sophists. Verbs and nouns apparently had already been distinguished, but Protagoras is said to have discovered the three genders of the Greek noun and three moods of the verb, indicative, imperative, and optative. In addition, he distinguished between question and answer, or interrogative and responsive propositions. We also meet with plenty of discussion of the meaning of single words and of passages in the poets; different interpretations of them are advanced in Plato and in Aristotle, and this must be obviously only a fraction of all that was going on at the time in conversation and in debate of which we have no record. These discussions will also raise the question whether the text of the poet discussed is correct, and textural criticism will move its first steps hesitantly, beginning with the text of Homer. Of the developments to which all these discussions give rise, the closest to literary criticism is rhetoric, and of course that is given over to taxonomy. Different types of speech are distinguished, in turn subdivided into other classes, and so forth. Basic to rhetoric is the distinction between the plain style and the ornate. All rhetoric may be said to deal with the varieties of which ornate style is capable. But, as Croce pointed out, this distinction has no genuine aesthetic foundation. The idea is that the plain style tells the thing as it is, while the ornate style adds something that makes it beautiful. But if the addition is made from the outside, i.e., if it does not connect intrinsically with the plain statement of the thing as it is, it is something factitious and artificial, detracting from the plain statement rather than enhancing it. If, on the other hand, it is something added intrinsically, it is part of the original statement, and not an ornament, but "a constitutive element of the expression, indivisible and indistinguishable in its unity."[12]

But the idea of the external ornament offered a wide opportunity for the taxonomist to rush in and multiply classifications and subdivisions of ornaments, metaphors, figures, and so forth. One rhetorician is said to have classified fourteen forms of metaphors, not to speak of the many forms of "figures of speech," such as ellipsis, pleonasm, metonymy, etc., etc. This kind of rhetoric flourished throughout antiquity, the Middle Ages and the Renaissance, but even in modern days we find critics like Northrop Frye distinguishing seven classes of imagery, four "pre-generic narrative elements of literature," six phases of tragedy, and so forth.[13] The attraction of taxonomy never ends for a certain type of mind.

There is a pretty philosophical parable, which I heard from Father D'Arcy, about a mad painter, who conceived the insane idea of painting a picture of the whole universe. Having provided himself with a canvas which he considered large enough for the purpose, he proceeded to put down every single thing in the universe on it. Finally he decided that he had completed his task, and looked back with satisfaction upon the finished picture. But then to his dismay he discovered that he had forgotten to include one thing in the picture which *was* in the universe, namely, himself. He proceeded to repair this omission in a small vacant corner of the picture, and painted himself making the celebrated painting of the universe. But his troubles were not yet over, as the reader may perhaps guess.

This might be considered somewhat similar to what happened to the Greek mind with the Sophists. After them, Greek speculation practically never recovered the lighthearted confidence of the early cosmologists, who knew precisely what the substance of the universe was, and unhesitatingly defined it. The Greek mind may be said to have never got over the jolt administered to it by the great Sophist Protagoras when, faced with the problem of finding a common measure for all things, a standard by which to evaluate everything, (something of the same order as the canvas of the mad painter), he proclaimed roundly: *"Man is the measure of all things, of those that are that they are, of those that are not that they are not,"* in fact, of Being and Not-being, those two great opposites of Greek speculation. Thus he made the first great statement of relativism in Western thought, but, although he contributed to the study of speech, as we saw, he does not seem to have applied his principle to the problems of literary criticism, where it could find a large field for application.

Socrates

Socrates is one of the most familiar figures in world history, and yet one of the most tantalizing personalities in the history of philosophy. Everybody knows what he looked like, his snub nose, protruding eyes, thick lips and short beard, as represented in a number of ancient portraits, more or less authentic. Familiar, too, is his fate: how he employed continual irony, which made him a gadfly to his fellow citizens who finally put him to death on a trumped up charge of irreligion, which makes him one of the first martyrs of free thought. Familiar also is his method or arguing, the so-called *elenchus,* by never advancing a positive statement, under profession of ignorance, and asking questions from his opponent, so leading him through a series of admissions until the unfortunate man found himself entangled in contradictory propositions. More constructively, perhaps, the Socratic method in teaching may be said to consist of drawing out of the pupil by a series of adroit questions, until he comes upon the true answer as if it were his own conclusion, and not something he has been taught by someone else.

All this is familiar enough; but Socrates, true to his method of interrogating rather than dogmatizing, did not leave a single written word. And here comes the tantalizing situation. For he had disciples (at least two) who knew

how to write and did write about him, i.e., Xenophon and
Plato. But although they relate much that is common to
both, yet they also differ, and on some important points.[14]
So we have to infer the real Socrates from a confrontation
of their writings, and of some other testimonies.[15]

Xenophon, who left some books on other subjects, was
more of a practical man than a philosopher, less original
and less profound than Plato, but a great admirer of Socrates. We might think that he should be more reliable and
matter-of-fact. But his Socrates, though an outstanding figure, has a rather commonplace mind, and may reflect the
limitations of the narrator. On the other hand, Plato was a
creative genius and a great constructive philosopher, but
how far can one trust him on matters of fact? Not much, for
he takes quite obvious liberties with facts, and in his later
dialogues makes Socrates, as practically all scholars now
admit, a mouthpiece for his own philosophy. Gregory
Vlastos, who has studied the question most recently in his
The Philosophy of Socrates, concludes that the early dialogues of Plato represent the real Socrates, but not the later.

However I will note a remarkable parallel (or anticipa-
tion or derivation)[16] of one of Plato's most important aesthetic doctrines in Xenophon's *Memorabilia of Socrates*
(3.10). Socrates is shown in conversation with the painter
Parrhasius, as he was fond of talking to craftsmen of all
sorts about their art or craft; and here he is actually expounding a positive doctrine, not practising an *elenchus.*
He defines painting as the "reproduction of visible objects,"
which by means of colors presents a likeness of the clear,
the concave, and so forth. This of course is the theory of
mimesis. But Socrates then goes on to say that painting
gathers from many objects the elements of human beauty,
in order to compose a whole that is more beautiful: "It
seems in portraying beautiful shapes, since it is not easy
to come upon one man whose features are all flawless, you
make wholly beautiful bodies by assembling from many the
most beautiful features of each" (3.10).

To this well-known argument it should be observed that any particular that becomes part of a synthesis loses any character it may have had before and acquires the character of the synthesis. So a beautiful composition need not be made out of beautiful words or beautiful phrases. Any word or phrase in an aesthetic synthesis will become a component of its total beauty, whether originally beautiful or not.

Plato

$\mathscr{D}$ With Plato we come not only to one of the greatest minds of antiquity but also to a writer of whom we possess the entire works in the complete text. We do not have to piece them out or make them out from fragments sparsely and almost accidentally preserved, as with the Pre-Socratics, but we can read him whole; and we even have some apocrypha. Other problems will arise, not a few, in connection with these works, but they will be problems in interpretation and not in reconstruction.

All the speculations of the earlier thinkers, Presocratics and Socratics, build up the foundation upon which Plato's edifice arises, not isolated like Stonehenge upon Salisbury Plain, but like the Acropolis rising above the city of Athens. The speculations on the one and the many, on the opposites and their unity, on being and becoming, on the limited and the unlimited, come up again in the thirty-six dialogues for a more profound and analytical treatment.

Take for instance the old dilemma of the one and the many. In the *Philebus,* Plato shows the way to its solution. Both concepts are valid and inseparable: "the one is the many . . .and the many are only one," "an identical unity being thus found simultaneously in unity and in plurality"

(14E, 15B).[1] And in the *Sophist*: "the real is both many and one" (242E).[2] Of course, the ultimate unity for Plato is the idea, which is a one that exists in and for a multiplicity of particulars, and about which we shall have something more to say later.

But from now on, Plato's solution to the dilemma has provided the foundation for later speculation. It is even implied in the passage from Emerson quoted in chapter 2 on the one and many. And from there it is only a step to pass to the concept of the Organic Unity which we find in the perfect work of art, and which consists of a number of parts (or details) reduced to unity, and of a unity made up of several parts. As it was put by a later thinker: "The parts are constituted by their dependence upon and in the whole, and yet the whole is composed by the addition of several parts together. Each extreme is what it is through the other. Only those parts can make up a whole, which somehow have the whole in them: and to become the whole, they must contrive to wholly obliterate their particular character."[13]

Furthermore, the observations of grammarians and rhetoricians on language and on texts all contribute something to Plato's doctrine. But when we come to his doctrines on art and on poetry, there is a fundamental remark of Zeller's to be recalled: "Plato has instituted no independent inquiries into the essential nature of Art or of the Beautiful any more than in that of the philosophy of religion. He always alludes to both, but always in connection with some other discussion; and what he says does not give us a very clear idea of their distinguishing characteristics. Because Plato himself was an artist, though a philosophic artist, he cannot be just to pure art. Because his general view of the world is at the same time aesthetical, he cannot discriminate sharply enough the object of art from that of philosophy—the Beautiful from the True and the Good."[4]

Nearly all of Plato's doctrines on art appear in some form in the *Phaedrus*. We will now consider this dialogue in detail. It begins as an intellectual comedy, then rises to a vision of the celestial and the superhuman, and finally concludes by returning to intellectual comedy. This makes it one of the most finished and variously fashioned dialogues of Plato.

The story is simple.[5] Socrates goes for a walk in the country—an unusual thing for him to do, city-bred and city-rooted as he is—together with his young friend Phaedrus. The latter is full of naïve enthusiasm for the "orator" Lysias, a writer who, as we see from his extant works, was something of a disciple of the Sophists and a prominent exponent of the newly developed art of rhetoric. His skill in argumentation was such that he could defend the most improbable or preposterous conclusions, and he was recently heard by Phaedrus arguing the paradox that a suitor not in love should be preferred to a suitor who is in love.[6] This kind of elaborate encomia of unworthy things was a fad of some ancient writers and was cultivated again in the Renaissance.[7] Furthermore, Phaedrus has with him the full text of the speech, or essay, in question. Socrates expresses an interest in the subject, and Phaedrus is only too pleased to read it out to him. So we have it in full, but whether it was a parody by Plato or an authentic composition of the historical Lysias is a matter for conjecture.[8]

The dialogue begins with a discussion of the art of composition, but the example given is rather contrived. Socrates nourishes higher standards, and has has something to say about poetry to this naïve admirer of Sophistical devices. He opens his criticism in a low key, finding fault only with the manner in which the subject is presented: it is repetitious, says the same things over and over, with different words but no difference in meaning. Phaedrus immediately leaps to the defense of his favorite, and replies that this is just the merit of the composition: it says all that can possibly be said on the subject, and even Socrates cannot find anything more to add to it. Socrates obligingly admits this, then crushingly observes that it is impossible to add to arguments that arise inevitably from the subject, and which therefore do not call for any special invention. (It has been noted Socrates has incidentally introduced here the critical distinction between the subject of a composition and the way it is treated, or content and form, a distinction which may have been already traditional at the time.)[9]

Socrates then rises to constructive criticism, and shows Phaedrus how the thing should have been. In fact, he rewrites the whole composition, an admirable exercise in writing (it is of course all done orally). The beginning, Socrates says, should have been the definition of the subject, and the following arguments should have been based on it—the Socratic-Platonic approach to reasoning here exemplified, and its principles theorized in the later 277B. The arguments for rejecting the sincere lover in favor of the non-lover should have been drawn from the definition of love. Socrates is about to do this, but he suddenly stops and gives up the whole discussion. Praising the non-lover has become abhorrent to him. Socrates explains that his familiar demon—that kind of guardian angel that prevents him from wrongdoing—has just checked him, so he will cease to blaspheme love. Instead, he embarks upon an entirely new discourse in praise of love (244 ff.). Sophistical paradox is thenceforth abandoned; Socrates now speaks out of deep conviction, and delivers one of his most eloquent and imaginative discourses, which cultimates in the vision of the empyrean where the eternal ideas reside, and where immortal souls also dwell before they are born to this world. Love is now seen as a kind of divine madness, by which the soul is freed from the restrictions of the body and rises to the contemplation of the divine idea of Beauty. From this point of view, love is seen to be akin to religious enthusiasm and to poetic inspiration (250). We have now touched the subject of poetry and will soon reach the subject of poetic unity.

Having shown how love is to be properly treated, Socrates turns back to another question raised by the discourse of Lysias, how to write well. He asks Phaedrus: "What then

is the way of writing well or badly?" To make it clear that
he is talking of the art of writing in its broadest sense, he
adds: "whether in a public or private document, in verse
as a poet or in prose as an ordinary man?" (258A). The
answer to this broad question is that a composition "should
be like a living being, with a body of its own as it were, and
neither headless nor feetless, with a middle and with members adapted to each other and to the whole" (246C, Jowett's
translation with slight changes). In the last part of the dialogue, the art of writing, after being defined in its broadest
sense, is narrowed down to rhetoric on one side (271D) and
to philosophy on the other (278B).

The quotation above introduces in criticism the principle
which we know as "organic unity," here apparently presented for the first time, but which from now on will have
a central place in poetic theory. This principle is sometimes
referred to as the organic "simile" or even the organic
"metaphor," particularly by critics who want to get rid of
principles in general and reduce all ideas to metaphors, and
thence to nonsense. But every word in the language is based
on a metaphor, including the word "metaphor" itself, which
originally stood for a "carry over." The organic unity principle can easily be distinguished from the accompanying
metaphor: the principle defines the relation of the parts to
the whole, using terms which are not derived from animal
life but more general, and the simile points to its analogy
in members of a living body, but they are not one and the
same. An important specification is also made here: the
relationship should be double, the relation of the parts to
the whole and the relationship of the parts to each other.

Let us examine this important passage even more closely
(key terms of the original are given in parentheses): "Every
discourse (λόγος) must be composed like (ὥσπερ), or in the
likeness of, a living being (ζῷον), with a body of its own, as
it were, so as not to be headless or feetless, but to have a
middle (μέσα) and members (ἄκρα) arranged in fitting (πρέπον)
relation to each other and to the whole (ὅλον)." It may be

noted that what is generally considered an essential point of organic unity is not mentioned here: i.e., that an alteration of a part, whether by addition or removal, involves the alteration of the whole, but it may be considered a corollary of it.

Then Socrates, to exemplify, quotes a short anonymous poem[10] which raises some other questions. It is an inscription on a statue placed near the fountain on the grave of the legendary king Midas. This little epigram, as it is called technically, is not without charm in the original. It may be that its Greek character gives it for us the attraction of the antique, but to Socrates it seems to have been just an inscription by the roadside, rather casually put together. I quote it in Hackforth's translation, which has the merit of being in verse like the original:

> *A Maid of bronze I stand on Midas' tomb.*
> *So long as waters flow and trees grow tall,*
> *Abiding here on his lamented grave*
> *I tell the traveller Midas there is laid.*

Now on this little composition Socrates makes the criticism that its lines can be read in any order, 1, 2, 3, 4 or 4, 3, 2, 1, or any other way without making any difference to the sense. Socrates goes on to point out that this also applies to Lysias's prose discourse: he "does not begin at the beginning," "the parts of the discourse are thrown out helter-skelter," "the second topic is not placed second for any good reason, nor any of the others." In other words, it is poorly composed.

Now this criticism suggests another way of looking at the relationship between parts of a composition not mentioned before: order, and the parts should be presented in their proper order. Order ($\tau\alpha\xi\iota\varsigma$) is brought up in other dialogues of Plato,[11] but it may be considered implicit in the original definition of organic unity.

Returning to Socrates' example of faulty composition, I cannot quite find it in me to condemn it, even if its lines are rearrangeable at will. Being short, each of its lines is complete, and no confusion is produced by rearrangement. Now this introduces the element of size: the shortness of the composition; and size is a point that Aristotle makes in his definition of beauty: "Beauty is a matter of order and size" (*Poetics* 1450B36), which also brings back "order" into it. Furthermore, it may be said that there is such a thing in poetry as progression through parallel statements. Each of the lines is complete in itself, but they all contribute something to the whole, which would suffer alteration if one of them were omitted—one of the marks of organic unity. The converse test would be would the poem be improved, or simply altered, by any addition to it? We need not cudgel our brains to invent new lines for it, since a Greek author has obligingly provided us with a version of this same epitaph with two more lines (Diogenes Laertius 1.6.21).[12] They add nothing to it, and appear mere padding. Hence the epigram would seem to satisfy the conditions for organic unity, in spite of Socrates' criticism of it. Each of its lines is in keeping with the others and with the whole, and any addition or diminution would hurt it.

In prose, particularly argumentative prose like Lysias's discourse, such looseness of structure is not to be tolerated. But in poetry, which is not logical argument, looseness is not necessarily bad, because much depends upon other factors. Nor does the parallel progression found in the epigram and in other compositions, some much later, as Walt Whitman's for example, involve complete lack of any form, and therefore does not really support some modern speculations about so-called "open form," for there is an inner cohesion to it. Organic unity turns out to be not a merely external "structure," for the outer arrangement would correspond to an inner connection, and the two should tally perfectly with each other. Such is the unity of form and matter.

In Socrates' definition the required relation of the parts receives an epithet: it should be "proper" (or fitting, (πρέπον). Now "proper" is a very general term, which can be particularized in several different ways, but it is not so particularized here. So the definition cannot be charged with being tautological. Socrates is not saying (as some modern upholders of the futility argument might say) that "beauty consists of a beautiful arrangement," which would indeed be tautological. He refers to the general structure of the arrangement, leaving its specific qualities open. For instance, "proper" might be defined as "adapted as a means to an end," which would make it consistent with an utilitarian aesthetic ("beautiful is what subserves a function"), such as is placed in the mouth of Socrates in other dialogues.[13]

To make it abundantly clear that this principle of organic unity applies not only to prose and to oratory but also to poetry of the highest kind, as tragedy is said to be in the *Gorgias* (502B), Socrates refers it explicitly to dramatic composition: "Suppose," says Socrates, "somebody were to come to Sophocles or to Euripides and to say he knows how to make a very long speech [even] about a small matter, and a short speech [even] about a great matter, and also a sorrowful speech, or any kind of speech, and in teaching this fancies that he is teaching the art of tragedy?" Phaedrus, who by this time has learnt his lesson, replies: "They too would surely laugh at him if he fancies that tragedy is anything but the arranging of those elements in such manner that will be suitable to each other and to the whole" (268C–D).

So tragedy is also subject to the law of organic unity. As here defined, its parts are the speeches of which it is made up. This may seem to be a rather inadequate analysis of tragedy. But within this narrow frame, Plato applies organicity to tragedy more definitely than does Aristotle in the *Poetics*. For Aristotle, as we shall see, found organicity only in one of the parts into which he analyzed tragedy, i.e., only to the plot or *mythos,* and did not apply organicity to the unification of all the parts into a single whole, but limited himself to making an enumeration of them, i.e., mere taxonomy, although stressing the preeminence of plot, which does not provide a synthesis.

Plato's organicism becomes the foundation for the criticism of contemporary rhetoric which occupies a sizeable part of the conclusion of the dialogue. The art of public speaking in a democratic state was much in demand and instruction in it paid well, so there were a host of teachers and handbooks were written analyzing all the devices of rhetoric and defining them with Greek subtlety. It was, as we say today, a technique. Socrates criticises this technique in the *Phaedrus* on the ground that it sets preestablished rules and prescriptions for all compositions, regardless of their subject, of the capacity of the author and of the nature of the audience. This survey is spiced with irony throughout.

PHAEDRUS: There is surely a great deal to be found in books on rhetoric.

SOCRATES: Yes, thank you for reminding me. The first point, I suppose, is that a speech should begin with a preamble: that is what you mean, the niceties of art?

PH.: Yes.

SOC.: And then comes Exposition, accompanied by Direct Evidence, thirdly Indirect Evidence, fourthly Probabilities; the great Byzantian word-maker also speaks of Confirmation and Supplementary Confirmation.

PH.: You mean the excellent Theodorus?

SOC.: Of course. And we are to have a Refutation and a Supplementary Refutation, both for the prosecution and for the defence. And we can't leave the admirable Evenus of Paros out of the picture, the inventor of Covert Allusion and Indirect Censure and (according to some accounts) the inventor of Indirect Censure in mnemonic verse? A real master, that. . . . And then

Polus: what shall we say of his *Muses' Treasury of Phrases* with his Reduplications and Maxims and Similes, and of words *à la Lycumnus* which that master made him a present of as his contribution to fine writing?

P H . : But didn't Progatoras in point of fact produce many such works, Socrates?

s o c . : Yes, my young friend, there is his *Correct Diction* and other excellent works. On the way to conclude a speech there seems to be general agreement, though some call it Recapitulation and others by some other name.[14]

It should be by now apparent that what Socrates is criticizing at this particular point (and possibly at this particular point alone) is the system of Rules, in this case the Rules for Fine Writing, which later, under the influence of Plato's disciple Aristotle, were extended to the writing of poetry and carried on to extremes in the so-called "Classical System of Poetics," which is pure taxonomy. Hence the uselessness of purely mechanical rules. Let us note in passing the adjective "mechanical," which more and more presents the opposite to "organic." Hence the elaborate systems of technical devices of the rhetoricians will teach no one to write well.

Then follows in the *Phaedrus* the positive doctrine: the subject of the composition should be the determining factor in making its divisions and planning their arrangement. The subject, we may add, as conceived by the mind of its author in all its particularity and idiosyncrasy, and not as an abstract scheme. So Socrates concludes that the rhetorician, at best, may be said to deal with the preliminaries of composition rather than with composition istelf (268E, 269A and C).

In the *Statesman* (299D–E) Plato argues again against general rules set up for the arts and crafts, specifically including "all the imitative arts, like painting" (299D). The term here translated "imitative" is "mimetic," which here appears to mean simply "figurative."

Plato ends the *Phaedrus* giving the right principles for argumentative writing, and his remarks cease to apply to poetics. He maintains that a good argument should be based on truth, not on a semblance of truth or on trickery, and truth is to be reached through the rational processes of analysis and synthesis, or *diaeresis* and *synagōge* (265D–E). Synthesis provides the definition of the subject to be discussed; analysis draws the divisions of the argument from the definition so provided. The two processes make up the art that Plato here calls "dialectic," thus starting the career of a term which was to have a vast future; and he adds that the whole of rhetoric is contained in them (269B). Now a similar argument may be made in poetics; the divisions of the poem discovered by analysis should be based on the subject—specifically, on the configuration of the poetic image, and not on its accessories or external relations; but Plato does not carry the method into poetics. Later Longinus will do it in his *Sublime* (on Sappho's ode, ch. 10).

There is another dialogue in which Plato refers to the principle of organic unity, but there he does not make use of the organic simile (which goes to show that this simile is not indispensable to the principle). The simile resorted to in the *Gorgias* is different (503E):

"The orator, like other craftsmen [δημιουργοί], has his own particular work in view, and thus selects the things he needs for that particular work, not at random, but with the purpose of giving a certain form [Εἶδος] to whatever he is working upon. For example, look at the painters [ζωγραφοί], the builders, the shipwrights, or any other craftsmen, to see how each arranges everything according to a certain order and makes each part fit with the other, until he combines the whole into a regular and well-ordered composition."

In these and previous statements, there is still a part of the definition of organic unity which is lacking—"any alteration of a part involves an alteration of the whole." This specification was made by Aristotle in the *Poetics* (1451A-32), and with a slight difference in the *Ethics*: "we often say of good works of art that it is not possible either to take away or to add anything" (1106A16). It has now become an integral part of the definition of organic unity, as we saw in the modern critics quoted at the beginning.

In these discussions of aesthetic unity the idea of the "whole" continually recurs. It is extended to the problems of medicine in the *Charmides* (156C–E). A doctor does not cure the head of the patient alone; he must also cure the rest of the body. In fact, he should treat "the whole and parts together," for "the part can never be well unless the whole is well." Another simile is used in the *Republic* (420D), that of the statue which of course is a work of art, and brings us back to aesthetics. The sculptor should "consider, whether, by giving this or that feature its due proportion, we make the whole beautiful." The simile is then applied to the idea of the perfect state.

The relation of the parts to the whole has given rise to a famous proposition, often repeated, that "the whole is more than the sum of its parts." This saying apparently originated in the solution given by Aristotle to a dilemma presented in Plato's *Theaetetus* (203–5). Socrates involves young Theaetetus in a series of dilemmas relating to the whole and the parts. In a complex object, is the sum of the parts, Socrates asks, more than the whole? If so, there is something in the whole which is not the parts. But if the parts constitute all that there is of a whole, and nothing else is added, then the whole can be nothing more than the sum of the parts.[15]

This was answered by Aristotle[16] in the *Metaphysics* (1041B12).[17] There he points out that there is something more in the whole than the parts:[18] that which holds them together. And that, according to Aristotle's general presuppositions, can only be form. It is form, in the Aristotelian sense, that makes the parts its matter, thus producing the individual thing or substance, which is the synthesis of form and matter. Now if the term *form* is given an aesthetic significance, going beyond Aristotle, we shall see how important for poetics Aristotle's solution can be, even though he did not use it in his own *Poetics*.

But before we pass on to Aristotle, there is another aspect of the *Phaedrus* to be observed. In spite of the fact that the main subject of the *Phaedrus* is not poetics, this dialogue is rich in aesthetic theories, including two of the most famous ones—the theory of poetic inspiration and the theory of ideal beauty. These two may be connected and held at the same time, but not necessarily so, and both independently and together they have played such a great role in subsequent speculation that they must be taken notice of.

The first theory, that of poetic inspiration, recurs more than once in the dialogues. It is of course in keeping with traditional Greek belief that a god, Apollo or a Muse, speaks through the lips of a poet. The theory of inspiration appears in the *Apology* (22B–C), in the *Meno* (99D) and in the *Laws* (719C). The latter passage is remarkable, because it seems to point to a conflict between inspiration and the other aesthetic doctrine current among the Greeks, and developed by Plato in *Republic,* books 1 and 3, namely that all art and literature are on "imitation" of reality, or *mimesis.*

The inspiration theory is introduced perhaps ironically in an early dialogue, the *Ion.* Socrates advances this theory to a conceited professional reciter of Homer, who believes that he cannot account for the superior beauty of his recitations except by some supernatural insufflation. Socrates, who is slowly deflating him, suggests that, like a poet, he receives power directly from a Muse.

In the *Phaedrus* poetry is definitely placed among the "divine frenzies" enumerated by Socrates; it is a *theia mania* (θεία μανία, 244): "There is a third form of possession or madness, of which the Muses are the source. This seizes a tender, virgin soul and stimulates it to rapt passionate expression, especially in lyric poetry, glorifying the countless mighty deeds of ancient times for the instruction of posterity. But if any man come to the gates of poetry without the madness of the Muses, persuaded that skill alone will make him a good poet, then shall he and his works of sanity with him be brought to naught by the poetry of madness, and behold, their place is nowhere to be found" (245A).[19] And later: "This is the best of all forms of divine possession, both in itself and in its sources, both for him that has it and him that shares therein; and when he that loves beauty is touched by such madness he is called a lover. Such a one, as soon as he beholds the beauty of this world, is reminded of true beauty" (249D). "Now beauty, as we said, shone bright among these visions, and in this world below we apprehend it through the clearest of our senses . . . sight" (250D).

The connection between the vision of the beautiful and the madness of the Muses, or poetry, is perhaps not absolutely tight, but it does not seem unreasonable to assume it. Also in the above passage there are hints of two other traditional Greek views about poetry, the didactic theory and the so-called monument theory, or the theory that the function of poetry is to praise great men.

Usually when Plato speaks of beauty he refers to physical or natural beauty rather than to the beauty of art, although he sometimes refers to the beauty of works made by *skilled* craftsmen. In the *Phaedo* (76B) the examples of beauty are "men, horses, clothes, and so on." In the *Hippias Major* (287E–288B, C) they are a maiden, a mare, a well-made pot; but a great work of art, the Athena of Phidias, is also mentioned (290A). In the *Republic* the parallel to the ideal state is found in "the most beautiful man" (472D). Beauty also belongs to pure geometrical forms, pure colors and pure sounds (*Philebus* 51C–D).

The idea of the beautiful includes an ethical element Socrates says, "the good, I assert, is beautiful" (*Lysis* 216D), "the good and the beautiful are the same" (*Banquet* 201C), and in the *Gorgias* Polus affirms, "Socrates, you have offered a fine definition of the beautiful in defining it by pleasure and good" (475A). Finally in the *Timaeus* (87C), "Everything that is good is *beautiful* and the *beautiful (kalón)* is not without proportion," thus including another facet of beauty—proportion or "measure" (*métron*). In the *Gorgias* (474D–E) laws, institutions, and music are all called beautiful. It is difficult to draw here a hard and fast line of division.[20]

More definite than the specific content of "the beautiful" is its metaphysical or ontological status. It is for Plato one of the eternal ideas. As he explains in the *Phaedo* (100D), "the one thing that makes an object beautiful is the presence or association with it, in whatever way the relation comes about, of absolute Beauty." What is absolute beauty? It is "that Beauty by which all beautiful things are beautiful." For we cannot say that something is beautiful unless we have some conception of beauty in our minds, and this conception must be objective and universal; that is, exist independently of our minds, and remain forever unchanging in itself.[21] The most pregnant description of it is perhaps in the *Symposium* 211E: "to see the beautiful itself, pure and unalloyed, uncontaminated and unmixed."[22] From this idea of beauty, seen mainly in works of nature and not in art, there developed in time the idea of the aesthetic beauty which is the goal of the artist, "the glorious prototype of beauty to which the artist, as a creator, may cast his eye."[23] The stages of this process were set forth in detail by Panofsky in the quoted work. This is the concept that enjoyed such a vogue in the Renaissance and in later ages, as Panofsky abundantly documents.

So far we have only skirted the theory of ideas, a complex subject upon which all discussions of Plato must turn; but perhaps a brief reference can be made to two basic questions relating to them upon which little is to be found in Plato himself: 1) How many are the ideas, which are they, and what relations subsist among the different ideas?[24] 2) How do the ideas relate to the divine mind? Are they thoughts in the mind of God, or do they subsist independently of it? The first of these alternatives has been called "intra-deical," the second "extra-deical."[25]

To a philosopher who believed in an eternal and immutable God, the theory of the eternal and immutable ideas raised the question of the relation of the ideas to God. The answer given was that the ideas are nothing else but the thoughts of God; so they exist in the mind of God, and are the eternal objects of God's eternal thinking. This answer preserved the prerogatives of both God and the ideas, and also, as has been noted,[26] replaced a system of abstract relations with the concept of mental activity, and marks a step forward.

This survey of the aesthetic theories in Plato will conclude with a quick look at what is the most notorious opinion expressed by Plato upon poetry, his exclusion of the poets from the ideal state described in the *Republic*. Socrates there argues, in a speech perhaps tinged with irony, that only certain poems, i.e., those relating unbecoming tales of the gods, have no place inside that state. Even these poems are not banned because of their art. It is not considered wrong to write poetry, but only poetry on certain subjects. Plato apparently excludes both epos and lyrical poetry from allowed subjects, and restricts the poems allowed in the *Republic* to "hymns to Gods and praises of just men" (607A), in keeping with the contentualistic and didactic trend already noted in philosophers like Heraclitus and Xenophones, of which there are other traces in Plato. This whole attitude is based on the mimetic theory of poetry developed in books 3 and 10 of the *Republic,* and which we have referred to already. Why this particular argument comes up at this point involves the discussion of the whole *Republic* and that we must renounce here.

So we have seen that there are several theories of beauty in Plato, and I will not attempt the difficult task of relating them to each other, for that involves the whole problem of Plato's philosophy as expounded in all his dialogues. Among these theories of beauty is the idea of organic unity which is our particular goal, and of which we have tried to trace the origin and the developments. The French scholar Robin emphasized its unifying character effectively as follows: "the unity of the essence of the Beautiful is not the unity of a collection, like that of an 'all,' but an indivisible unity: the Beautiful is only that which it is, and as such it has never ceased to be one with itself."[27]

The concept of organic unity, when fully developed by later speculation, will reveal itself as the concept of the subjective activity of the human mind, in contrast to the objective view which prevails in ancient thought. Yet even in Plato there is at least a hint of the subjective view in a passage in the *Theaetetus,* where Plato makes what is perhaps his greatest advance in the direction of subjectivity (185B). There he is refuting the empiricist doctrine that all knowledge comes through the senses. Socrates acknowledges that colors are only known through sight, and sounds through hearing, but how do we get to know what is common to both? E.g., that they both exist and that they are distinct from each other, or the thought of them "as together two, while each is one: it cannot be by the agency of either sight or hearing singly that one forms a conception that thus embraces both."[28]

This may be called Kant in embryo or, the gist of the Transcendental Analytic of the *Critique of Pure Reason*: All sensuous impressions are received from outside, but their sifting, classification and organization is operated by the mind. Having got that far, Plato immediately swung back to his objective point of view: the common elements in sensation are things like "existence and non-existence, likeness and unlikeness, and also unity and number in general" (185C). These, as Cornford pointed out, are no other than Plato's eternal ideas, that do not owe their existence to mind, but are completely independent of it.[29]

5

A Cursory Glance at the Scholarship
on *Phaedrus* 264C

The conclusion that this passage of the *Phaedrus* presents for the first time a basic concept of aesthetics and is therefore important for the general history of that discipline and of critics may meet, as experience has shown me, with two different and contradictory responses. The first is that this interpretation makes too much of what is only a secondary passage in the dialogue, hence quite properly slighted by students of Plato. The other claims that everybody knows already about this passage. So we will now give a rapid glance at the scholarship on the *Phaedrus,* and we shall note which critics have taken notice of the passage and how they have evaluated it, and which critics have not. At the end I shall offer some tentative conclusions to this cursory and incomplete survey.

One question which is indeed much debated by critics of the dialogue is what is its main subject. So many and so important theories are brought in: the theory of ideas, the doctrine of reminiscence, the correlative doctrine of the preexistence and reincarnation, the theory of love (more fully developed in the *Symposium*) and the discussion of rhetoric, relating to what Taylor designates "prose style" (p. 299). Nobody has argued that organic unity is its main subject, nor do I. Hackforth has dismissed the question of the main subject with the remark: "Plato does not write treatises, but dramatises arguments" (p. 9). Yet he does find a "dominant purpose" in it, which is "to vindicate the pursuit of philosophy" (ibid.). Whatever the main subject, critics agree that the other theories presented are not un-related. They may be said to converge on the theory of ideas, and even the organic parallel is an instance of that unity in multiplicity which constitutes one of the main fea-tures of the ideas.

As to the actual movement of the dialogue, it presents a highly artistic alternation of rise, climax, and descent. This is done through the instrumentality of only two characters, Socrates and an admiring interlocutor, but in an unfamiliar setting, which contributes to the unique artistic effect of the whole. Through this medium Plato was able to present a variety of tones in a unified artistic manner.

Now there are two recent critical surveys of studies on Plato, both published around 1960. One is vast, compre-hensive, and encyclopedic, the other is limited to a selection of important works which it analyzes singly. The first is by Harold Cherniss, "Plato (1950–1957)" in *Lustrum* 4 (1959) and 5 (1960), 2 vols. (Göttingen, 1960–61). It is arranged as a systematic classification of subjects found in both books and papers, fully indexed, and covers not only it professed limits (1950–57), but also the immediately preceding years, so that practically every contribution since 1930, if "rel-evant" (p. 471), and up to the early months of 1959, is included. At the beginning, Cherniss lists what he considers the three outstanding books of the period, "The works of Friedländer [P., *Platon* (Berlin, 1928–30)], Shorey [P., *What Plato Said* (Chicago, 1933)] and Stefanini [L., *Platone,* 2d ed., 2 vols. (Padua, 1949)]" (p. 11). We shall see something of each of these in turn.

The scond survey is Ernest Moritz Manasse, "Bücher über Platon," *Philosophische Rundschau,* 2 vols. (Tübingen, 1957–61). Volume 1 covers books in German, and volume 2 books in English. This is a series of thoughtful book reviews, rather than a systematical repertory, like the first. Both are useful in their different ways.

We will begin this survey with the German thinker who is generally considered to have marked the beginning of the modern critical study of Plato, Friedrich Schleiermacher (1768–1834). In 1804 he began publishing his translation of Plato, accompanied by critical introductions, which contain some of his most profound writing on Plato, even if his chronology is questioned. The first dialogue translated was the *Phaedrus,* precisely because he considered it Plato's earliest, a theory now generally abandoned. The dialogue, as Schleiermacher himself points out, is a work of consummate art; and it does not now seem likely (apart from other reasons) that Plato should have begun his dialogues with such a mature achievement. Schleiermacher also devoted considerable attention to the question, touched upon above, of what is its primary subject, and he concluded that it is the Platonic dialectic, supporting this thesis with a number of observations at the beginning of which he brings in the organic principle. For if, as some think, the main subject was love, "this beautiful work, worked up as it evidently is with the greatest pains, would appear deformed in a most revolting manner, utterly controverting the maxim that it must be fashioned like a living creature, having a body proportioned to the mind, and with parts also in due proportion. For the whole of the second part [which deals with rhetoric] would then be nothing but an appendage strangely tacked on and not even tolerably well fitted."[1] The speeches on love in their first part are introduced mainly for their manner and not for their subject, as instances of ways of writing, and that leads on to "the subject of the second part . . . the true nature of the art of speaking" (p. 51). That for Plato involves the art of thinking, i.e., dialectic (p. 58), by the method of definition and division treated in 265D ff., and so to the rejection of the superficial and even fraudulent art of the rhetoricians and sophists.

So Schleiermacher was well aware of the aesthetic value of the principle of organic unity, though he does not note that Plato extends it to poetry, and particularly to the art of tragedy. Nor does he follow it up in all its later critical developments, which actually were in full swing in his own day and reached a climax in the philosophy of Hegel.

In 1820 Hegel gave for the first time his course of lectures on aesthetics, and lectured again on the subject in 1823, 1826, and 1829.[2] After Hegel's death in 1831, notes from these lectures were put together and edited, not too brilliantly, by his disciple Hotho in 1835. In 1931 these notes were edited again, much more carefully, from the original manuscript by Georg Lasson; the text reads much better and it is more agile.[3] But after the first volume nothing more seems to have appeared of this edition; so I shall refer to the already cited earlier version of Osmaston (see n. 2) which may not be without errors but is complete.

Hegel being the philosopher who has developed most intensely the organic character of the Absolute and of its concept, which for him are one and the same thing, or the idea, we would expect him to introduce organic unity also in his aesthetics. And so he does, but he did not see it in Plato. On Plato he has only this to say in this work: that Plato condemned Homer and Hesiod for their anthropomorphic view of the deity (1:141), and that Plato's main merit as a philosopher is having made the essence of reality consist in the idea. But he also finds that Plato's essence is an "empty" or "abstract" universal, and not the concrete universal of Hegel's own philosophy, which might be approximately described as a universal, or general essence, embodied in a particular reality (1:27, 28, 197). However, Hegel acknowledged that the science of the beautiful begins with Plato (1:28). This he develops in his lectures on the history of philosophy,[4] showing that for Plato the essence of beauty is intellectual, the idea manifesting itself in the phenomenal world (2:273–74). But there is nothing on *Phaedrus* 264C.

Shortly after Hegel, a scholarly history of the ancient theory of art was written by Eduard Müller,[5] but not from the Hegelian point of view. It is a comprehensive survey of the ideas on aesthetics put forward by the ancient philosophers, critics, and poets or artists. It considers Plato "the founder of a theory of art from a political-ethical point of view" (1:27 ff.). Müller divides Plato's ideas into two main subdivisions: art as it is, and art as it should be. To the *Phaedrus* there are several references, but not to 264C. Organic unity might have found a place here, but it did not.

In 1868 the English scholar W. H. Thompson published an edition of the *Phaedrus* with a commentary[6] in which 264C is noted and related to other passages in Plato, not closely relevant, and in other Greek writers:[7] "This comparison of a well arranged discourse to a living creature occurs again in *Philebus* 64B. It is also implified *infra* 268C [i.e., the passage on tragedy]. Compare *Politicus* 177B." The *Philebus* passage is a general comparison and not specifically aesthetic. Socrates concludes a discussion saying, "to me it seems that the present debate we have produced an incorporeal ordered system for the control of a body in which a soul dwells." The *Politicus* passage compares an imperfect definition to "an outline sketch . . . still to be painted in colors." Thompson took note of the passage, but referred it only to rhetoric (p. 103).

Eduard Zeller's *History of Greek Philosophy* is a monumental work which marks the real beginning of the modern historical study of ancient philosophy. Its first volume made its appearance in 1844 with the title *Philosophie der Griechen: eine Untersuchung über Charakter, Gang und Hauptmomente ihrer Entwicklung.* The work, comprising three parts, was rewritten for the second edition and given a new title: *Die Philosophie der Griechen in ihrer geschichtlichen Entwicklung,* in several volumes (1856–68). Zeller went on making additions and revisions to his work all his life, giving an account of all later contributions, either in books or by papers, so that the work became an indispensable survey of scholarship, besides providing a profound historical interpretation. After his death in 1908, the work was kept up to date by successive scholars in later editions.[8] It was translated into several languages. The first volume of those translated into English was *Plato and the older Academy,* by S. F. Alleyne and A. Goodwin (London, 1876), and to that we shall refer henceforth. A new translation and updating was begun in Italy by R. Mondolfo in 1932. Several volumes have appeared by several editors, and the work is still in progress.

Zeller's account of Plato follows an approach then prevalent: his object is the "system" of Plato, the one system assumed to underlie all the extant dialogues, which he systematically expounds in its supposed structure, with subdivisions according to subjects and not according to dialogues. The more modern approach is to give up, for the time being at least, any such attempt, and to arrange the exposition according to the dialogues, in their most probable chronological order, with an eye to the development of Plato's thought and its changes in time (a problem which even Zeller has to cope with in chapter 3). Zeller's main exposition is according to the three "divisions" of the "system": i.e., Dialectic, Physics, and Ethics, with a "propedeutic" chapter on Plato's method in general, a subsequent chapter on "Plato's Views on Religion and Art," and a final chapter on *The Laws.*

So aesthetics comes to occupy a small corner in the system, and this is further restricted by Zeller's discussion of it. Besides beauty, which is the object of art, Plato recognizes a special "mental activity from which it proceeds. . . . but what he says about it is still far removed from an exact investigation and precise definition of the nature of fancy" (i.e., in English terminology, of the nature of the imagination). He summarizes adequately Plato's views on inspiration, on *mimesis* (p. 508), and on the moral effects of art (pp. 510–13). The exposition is rounded out by an account of artistic genres in Plato (pp. 513–14) and of rhetoric (pp. 514–16).

As always, Zeller's exposition is buttressed by a solid array of footnotes giving the location of the various passages cited, and references to the literature of the subject. The *Phaedrus* passage finds its place in the account of rhetoric and is lumped with the reference to "*Phaedr.* 259E–266C," p. 514, n. 99. This is all that Zeller has to say about it. Since his plan eschews the analysis of single dialogues, the *Phaedrus* passage 264C is lost sight of in the general system and buried in the account of rhetoric.

Zeller's idea of a system of Plato, to be drawn from the dialogues, had some share in his conclusion that the most constructive dialogues, *Republic* and *Laws,* were chronologically the last written, and all the others in which little is built up and much is questioned, doubted, or refuted, belong to the formative period of Plato, before he had reached final conclusions. To support this thesis, he analyzed the ideas expressed in each dialogue, and sought connections and developments between them. This method of internal analysis was challenged by Ueberweg (1861), who preferred "external" evidence, such as the references by Aristotle and the allusions to contemporary events, and many other interpretations were presented. At last an objective method for chronology was discovered, so-called stylometry, and developed especially by Lutoslawsky. This is now generally accepted; it places the so-called dialectic dialogues after the *Republic,* and the latter in something like a middle place in Plato's development, the *Laws* being his very last work.[9]

In this area Zeller has been definitely superseded. On the other hand, he has probably the merit of having laid the ghost of the interpretation that the ideas for Plato are thoughts in the mind of God—the intradeical interpretation, as Wolfson called it, which still had followers in Zeller's day, although it had already been rejected by Leibniz and others. From now on I shall not keep to a strict chronological order, since several works, like Zeller's, go through more than one edition, and I shall only be able to quote one.

In 1877 a great classical scholar, A. Boeck, in his *Encyclopaedia and Methodology of Classical Studies,* defined a work of literary art by prominently using the *Phaedrus* passage, and even went beyond it: "A work of literary art is, as Plato observed [*Phaedrus* 264], an organism; and in an organism the whole is prior to the parts. In effect the artist has the whole of his work before his mental eyes, as a single intuition as yet undeveloped, out of which the single parts then emerge [*herausbilden*] as organs of the whole. The individuality of the writer is concentrated in this unity of the work and must be grasped by the specific critical interpretation and followed in the further organization that follows."[10] Few classical scholars elsewhere, or afterwards, have shown such a grasp of aesthetics.

In 1883 appeared the first edition of Marcelino Menendez y Pelayo's *Historia de las ideas estéticas en España,* one of the fullest histories of the subject, which went through several editions, and is variously divided in the volumes of each edition. This work of wide learning and gracious presentation covers much more than the title indicates: its first volume is dedicated to ancient thought, Greek and Roman, while later there is a whole volume on German aesthetics. In the first volume the author expounds the aesthetics of Plato and duly translates *Phaedrus* 264C,[11] but refers it to rhetorical prose only and does not refer to its broader historical significance.

In 1887 Emile Egger published his *Essai sur l'histoire de la critique chez les Grecs* in Paris, referring to other passages of the *Phaedrus* but not to 264C. In 1887 also appeared Charles Bénard's *Aristotle*[12] which defines the Platonic idea as the "unité variée qui, dans son emploiement harmonieux engendre la diversité, la multiplicité (v. Parménide, Philèbe)," and provides philosophy with the concept of synthetic unity, but not specifically aesthetics.

In 1888 the French scholar Antoine Edouard Chaignet, author of several works on ancient thought, in his *Rhétorique* noted Plato's parallel between "discours" and a living being and admirably developed it:[13] "Le discours, oeuvre d'art humain, est semblable à un corps formé par la nature, organisé et vivant, ayant en soi son principe de vie et d'organisation. L'organisation est la tendance à l'unité par la coordination et la subordination des parties, qui deviennent des organes lorsque chacune d'elles a sa fonction propre et concourt à la fonction générale du tout" (pp. 353–54). But this is limited to "le discours," presumably in prose, and presented under "rhetoric." There is no reference to the *Phaedrus* as the origin of the idea. Similarly in 1893 J. Walter in his history of ancient aesthetics expounds *Phaedrus* 264C, but refers it to discourse (*die Rede*) and not to poetry.[14]

S. H. Butcher, best known for his translation and commentary of Aristotle's *Poetics* (New York, 1907) which we shall see in the following chapters, wrote previously a survey entitled "Greek Literary Criticism,"[15] where he presented fully and clearly the significance of *Phaedrus* 264C. After quoting the whole passage, Butcher says: "Here, observe, and for the first time, the law of internal unity is enunciated, as a primary condition of literary art—now commonplace, then a discovery . . . Organic as distinct from mechanical unity; not the homogeneous sameness of a sandheap, but a unity combined with variety, a unity vital and structural, implying mutual dependence of all the parts, such that if a part is displaced or removed, the whole is dislocated. . . . From this point of view the unity and artistic beauty of a literary composition are found to reside in a pervasive harmony, a single animating and controlling principle" (pp. 192–93).

He then gives an interesting side glance to literatures outside the classical tradition: "So said the Greeks and so we say. But every people has not shared this view," and he considers an instance of poetic unity conceived in a different way: "a Persian ode is made of couplets and independent of each other without continuity of discourse: and its unity derives only from common metre and common theme, like 'pearls upon a string' " (p. 193). This is not very different from a sonnet sequence in Western literature, where each sonnet is complete in itself. The whole sequence may present a higher unity in a general theme, but that can only be determined for each sequence, since some make no claim to such unity, some claim it and do not possess it. Goethe and Schiller's *Xenia* are independent couplets, epigrams mostly, and each has its own measure of poetic unity.

Butcher opened up another argument when he went on to say that "moderns" require "varying degrees of unity in different forms of literature:" e.g., the epic genre possesses "spacious compass"; and he referred to Aristotle's *Poetics,* chapters 18, 23, and 24. That introduced the division into genres, which Plato did not take too rigidly when he wrote the *Phaedrus,* where organic unity is predicated of the tragic genre without qualification, as we saw. The whole question of genres, which involves ultimately a different view of the essence of poetic art, will be taken up when we consider the *Poetics,* when I will discuss what Butcher has to say of the *Poetics* in the sentences omitted from the above quotations.

Finally, Butcher also noted Plato's use of the idea of the whole, noted here earlier, and he referred to *Laws* 10.903 B–C, where "Plato applies the principle of organic unity to the moral government of the world" (p. 192, n. 3). Butcher's essay had an immediate effect on its first appearance. It was referred to by Saintsbury in the first volume of his *History of Criticism* (1900): "It is nearly certain that, as Professor Butcher thinks, no one had anticipated him in the recognition of the organic unity necessary to a work of literary, as of all, art."[16]

Gomperz in his history of Greek philosophy also noted that "the comparison of a work of literature to an organism appears here for the first time (*Phaedrus,* 264C)," following

Thompson (1868).[17] In 1903 Sandys in his history of classical scholarship noted *Phaedrus* 268C with the comment, "Tragedy, in brief, has to be an organic whole,"[18] but he does not refer to the earlier, more general statement of 264C. Similarly Bosanquet in his history of aesthetics (2d ed., 1904) ascribes to Plato the concept of the organic unity of tragedy. "He pointed out that tragedy is an organic whole, and not a string of speeches expressive of various morals," referring to *Phaedrus* 268. Earlier he had said, "the relation of the whole to part—a slightly more concrete expression for unity in variety—has never been more perfectly elucidated and more justly appreciated than by Plato and Aristotle" and refers to *Phaedrus* 268D.[19]

In 1902 the first edition of Croce's *Aesthetic* appeared (it had reached the 9th ed. in its author's lifetime in 1950), which contains in part 2 a history of the subject twice as long as the exposition of his own theory (part 1). While his theory is strongly organic in its most mature form, as we shall see, Plato in part 2 appears only for the conception of ideal beauty and the condemnation of poets.[20] Wilamowitz in the second edition of his monograph on Plato has a section on the *Phaedrus,* with only a brief reference to the organic metaphor in 264C.[21] E. E. Sikes discusses Plato's views on poetry, but does not refer to *Phaedrus* 264C.[22] Friedländer in the second edition of his monograph on Plato limits the *Phaedrus* passage 264C to the "Bau der Rede" or structure of the discourse with no specific reference to its application to poetry.[23]

Rhys Roberts, in his compact book entitled *Greek Rhetoric and Literary Criticism* (1928), was emphatic in his recognition. "Another great conception of the *Phaedrus* is that every discourse should be like a living thing, with body, head and feet of its own, and with all its members adapted to one and to the whole: a 'literary drive'—the compelling instinct of authorship—should make each speaker or writer shape the several parts of his discourse into the organic and vital unity of artistic composition." Roberts then pro-

ceeds to relate this to Plato's principle of ideal beauty—
that love and that beauty which vivify the *Phaedrus*—and
refers to the heavenly vision.[24]

In 1939 Jaeger began publishing his outstanding history
of Greek culture, which in its third volume firmly assigns
to *Phaedrus* 264C the origin of the basic concept of organic
unity in poetics. "These are penetrating discoveries about
the nature of literary composition, which were taken up by
later writers, and became fundamental principles of classical poetic and rhetorical theory. It is important for us
to realize this: the principle that a work of literature must
be an organic unity was laid down by a philosopher, not by
a rhetorical critic of art, not by a poet; and its enunciator
was a philosopher who was also an artist, who admired natural organic unity and was also a genius."[25]

Luigi Stefanini's *Platone*[26] is probably the most extensive
philosophical study of Plato in all his works. It was recognized by Cherniss as one of the three outstanding books on
Plato published in the last fifty years.[27] Stefanini adopts
wholeheartedly the aesthetic concept of organic unity from
the *Phaedrus,* affirming again and again in his preliminary
appreciation of the dialogue[28] that it comes up to its own
standard, and defends it against a critic who found it faulty
in composition. But he does not take it up again in his detailed analysis of the dialogue, the unity of which he places
in the idea of the irrational through a subtle and complex
analysis which it is impossible to summarize fairly.[29]

In 1934 J. W. H. Atkins began a comprehensive history
of literary criticism in England which never went beyond
the eighteenth century (1951), but which began with two
volumes on antiquity. In the first of these, where Plato is
discussed, occurs this clear and emphatic passage. "Among
the outstanding principles of art revealed in his writings
none however is more illuminating than that principle of
organic unity which he regarded as one of the primary
conditions of art. The most familiar of his pronouncements
on this point occurs in the *Phaedrus* (264C), where he states

that 'every discourse (*lógos*) ought to be constructed like
a living creature.' Here it will be noticed, he requires not
only the unity or completeness that is provided by a suitable
beginning, middle, and end, but also a unity that was vital
in kind, all parts being related as the parts of a living organism, so that nothing could be omitted or changed without
injury to the whole. It was, in brief, a revelation of the
fact that artistic beauty resides in unity of effect, in a single
animating principle. . . . Nor is the doctrine limited by
Plato to matters of discourse or oratory." Quoting the other
passages, he concludes: "There can thus be no doubt that
the doctrine of artistic unity was regarded by Plato as of
universal application. He was, in fact, the first to bring to
light the logic of art, and what is more important, those
vital relations involved in organic unity."[30]

In the history of aesthetics by Gilbert and Kuhn[31] there
is no discussion of organic unity, but the passage in *Phaedrus* 264C is interpreted as follows: "A good speech is like
an animal skilfully carved at the joints, so that the natural
articulation of the creature is respected," and in poetry "the
reigning tone of the whole" is recognized (p. 54). J. G.
Warry (1962)[32] follows Bosanquet in his recognition of
"unity in variety" (p. 13) and in the *Phaedrus* sees mainly
Plato's theories on "sublimated passion" (p. 28). He acknowledges that "what is said here concerning literary
values is of considerable interest" (p. 25) but does not
elaborate. He seems to find the idea of organic unity more
in Aristotle (p. 88). Grube's *Greek and Roman Critics*
(1965) quotes the *Phaedrus* passage on the organic unity required in tragedy (p. 59), but not its general definition at
264C. But he does refer to it in the *Encyclopedia of Philosophy,* 1973, 3:499. A. E. Taylor in his well-known monograph on Plato (1926) which reached a fourth edition in
the thirties, gives due attention to the *Phaedrus,* but likewise
limited the organic simile to discourse. "A good discourse
ought to have a definite organic structure, just like a living
creature. There should be a definite plan underlying it

which should be ruined if you inverted the order of the paragraphs."[33] Grube's more recent book on Plato (1935) in its chapter on art refers to the condemnation of the Midas epitaph in the *Phaedrus* 264D: "wherein the order of the lines is quite immaterial. This is bad art." Lysias's speeches are likewise criticized for having "no form or structure. Everything is pell-mell and any one thing might be said before the other."[34]

The latest study of the *Phaedrus* by R. Hackforth (1952) contains a translation, a running commentary to the dialogue, and footnotes to the text. It is a most thorough study of the *Phaedrus,* but it has not got a single note to passage 264C, and as to the whole section in which it occurs, this is what the commentary has to say about it. "The last of this section (264A–D) is of relatively small importance: it does not bear upon the question of Lysias' knowledge or ignorance, but upon his style and argument: those things are of course matters of τέυη but, as we might put it, of τέχνη that is purely literary, not its philosophical aspect: though indeed from the way in which Socrates speaks at 264A4–6 it may be inferred that Plato thought of the two aspects as closely connected."[35] So the whole passage for Hackforth "is of relatively small importance"; it might have had importance if it had discussed Lysias's knowledge or ignorance, but it deals only with matters "purely literary," though literature and philosophy appear connected at 264A4–6. These are not the lines in which organic unity is defined, but a criticism of Lysias's order of topics. They are so translated by Hackforth himself. "No: he doesn't seem to get anywhere near what we are looking for: he goes about like a man swimming on his back, in reverse, and starts at the end instead of the beginning" (p. 128). There is not a word in Hackforth's book about organic unity, though plenty on the other topics of the dialogue.

In 1960, Paul Vicaire dedicated a full study of all of Plato's contributions to literary criticism. Among many other things, he noted and emphasized Plato's affirmation

of organic unity in the *Phaedrus,* following Atkins and
Jaeger, whom he refers to. It is important, he said, "that it
should be he, the philosopher, who has most definitely, if not
for the first time, formulated the principle according to
which a literary work should constitute an organic unity."
He also noted that Plato specifically extended the standard
of organic unity to tragedy. "Tragedy, like any other composition, requires a harmonious organisation of its elements
that will respect their mutual relations as well as the
whole."[36] At about the same time, Wladislaw Tatarkiewicz
published his history of aesthetics which was translated in
1970 and is the fullest work on the subject up to date, cover-
ing all periods and the theories of all the arts. He fully
reports the *Phaedrus* passage. "The 'rightness' of a work of
art depends, first of all, upon the proper arrangement of
parts, an internal order and a good structure. It has to have
an adequate 'beginning, middle, and end' to be similar to a
living being, to an organism which cannot be 'without
either head or feet'; it must have a middle and extremities
so composed as to suit each other and the whole work."[37]
Two German works on ancient aesthetics published in the
early sixties do not make any reference to the *Phaedrus*
passage.[38]

Harold Osborne in his *Aesthetics and Art Theory, An
Historical Introduction* (London, 1968) skimmed over
Phaedrus 264C, which he restricts to rhetoric and the art
of speech, and misses entirely on tragedy (pp. 191–92). In
1972 Whitney J. Oates in *Plato's View of Art* (New York,
1972), quoted in full *Phaedrus* 264C as a description of how
to "compose a particular work . . . in a way that it will
possess an organic unity" (p. 37). In 1972 Stanley E. Fish
included the *Phaedrus* in what he called self-consuming
artifacts (*The Experience of Seventeenth-Century Literature,* Berkeley, 1972). He quoted 264C as "the definition of
a good discourse," but did not note that it is a definition of
poetry (p. 9).

A full account of the study and commentaries on the

Phaedrus for the last century or so would prove interesting and instructive, from the point of view of the history of criticism as well as of the history of philosophy; but it must be left to other, better equipped scholarship. From our own rapid survey of the discussion of the passage 264C, we may perhaps conclude that while its significance was recognized, by and large, by the historians of criticism from Menendez y Pelayo to Saintsbury and from Atkins to Jaeger who saw the dialogue in the perspective of the general development of ideas, it was missed by a number (not by all) of the authors of monographs on Plato or on the *Phaedrus,* their attention being concentrated on their immediate object and not on its later influence.

6

Aristotle

Aristotle was Plato's greatest disciple and his greatest critic. He developed a fully rounded system that embraced all the philosophical disciplines—Ethics, Logic, Metaphysics, etc., as well as Poetics and Rhetoric—some of which derive their very names from the titles of the works he dedicated to them, thus bearing a lasting Aristotelian stamp. In them, Aristotle usually started from some Platonic theory, and then proceeded to give a revised version of it from a somewhat different point of view, which may be roughly and provisionally described as more "realistic" than Plato's "idealistic" views, especially in the matter of the ideas. Aristotle's objection to Plato's ideas was directed against their independent existence as separate objects, apart (*chorís*) from the world of experience. On the value of both these avenues to knowledge, the empirical as well as the speculative, Aristotle, in spite of being a great metaphysician, was strong.[1] He believed ultimately not in ideas but in substances (*ousíai*), or realities made up of form and matter. As Panofsky put it: "Aristotle healed the dualism between the world of Ideas and the world of appearances epistemologically by means of the synthetic interaction between the universal concept and the individual represen-

tation, and metaphysically by means of the synthetic interaction between Form and Matter. 'Everything comes out of
the substratum and the Form.' All that comes either from
Nature or from the hand of man no longer consists of the
imitation of a certain Idea by a certain appearance, but the
entrance of a certain Form into a certain matter."[2]

With these and other premises in his general outlook,
Aristotle wrote his work entitled *Poetics*. This book is a
priceless record of some of Aristotle's thoughts on a subject of capital importance to the Greeks and to us, and we
could not, nor would not, be without it. It has a lasting
place in the history of thought upon the problems of literature and has exercised an immense influence on criticism.
Every time I look into it—and I have been going through
it once a year for the past twenty years or so—I find something in it, some definition or distinction, or some other
detail that I had not noticed before. One reason for that
is that the book is written in a very elliptical style which
tends to obscure particulars, an elliptical style which was
brilliantly described and conveyed with particular cogency
by Gilbert Murray in a passage to which we shall return.[3]

Furthermore, Aristotle improves upon Plato in this respect, that his views are presented directly to the reader, and
not left to be inferred from a dialogue between more or less
fictitious characters. (Aristotle's own early dialogues are
now mainly lost.) For all these reasons the *Poetics* are to
be prized. But there is one serious shortcoming in this work
—its fragmentary condition. Since this does not seem to be
universally taken in, I will give the statements thereupon
by highly respected scholars. First, the great nineteenth-
century historian of Greek philosophy, Eduard Zeller: "Our
text shows many smaller or greater gaps, as also interpola-
tions (as ch. 12 and many smaller ones) and inversions (the
most considerable that of ch. 15 [on plot][4] which ought to
come after ch. 18 [also on plot]), which sufficiently prove
that we only possess Aristotle's work in a mutilated and
hopelessly corrupt condition."[5]

Gilbert Murray, a modern humanist, and a sincere admirer of Aristotle, said of the *Poetics*: "For one thing the treatise is fragmentary. It originally consisted of two books, one dealing with Tragedy and the Epic, the other with Comedy and other subjects. We possess only the first. For another, even the book we have seems to be unrevised and unfinished. The style, though luminous, vivid, and in its broader division systematic, is not that of a book intended for publication. Like most of Aristotle's extant writing, it suggests the M.S. of an experienced lecturer, full of jottings and adscripts, but never intended as a whole for the general reader. Even to accomplished scholars, the meaning is often obscure, as may be seen by a comparison of the three editions recently published in England, all the work of savants of the first eminence [Butcher, 1898, Bywater, 1909, and Margoliouth, 1911], or still more strikingly, by a study of the long series of misunderstandings and overstatements and corrections which form the history of the *Poetics* since the Renaissance."[6]

A recent historian of Greek aesthetics puts it thus: the *Poetics* "has reached us in a mutilated and incomplete condition. Although the work itself is invaluable for the profundity of its suggestiveness and acuteness of its distinctions, it remains a fragment to be eked out by whatever references to the subject can be gleaned from other Aristotelian treatises."[7]

And this is the work that generations of critics have regarded as the definitive treatise on poetry, as a perfectly constructed theory of aesthetics, and a sure guide to the critic in the evaluation of all poetry—something of the same status as Euclid's *Elements*![8] To react by calling *Poetics* just a heap of contradictions would be excessive, but it would not be entirely unjustified to call it an assemblage of loosely bound discrepancies. Nor is Aristotle to be criticized for this. Apollo Palatine only knows what the original work was like, of which the *Poetics* is only a remnant. So let us by all means learn from Aristotle what he can still teach us on metaphysics and on logic, on ethics, on politics and other subjects; let philosophers take up again his epistemology, if they think they can do so, after Hume and Kant. But let us give up futile attempts to bring the fragments of the *Poetics* into a coherent theory, for that is a lost cause. Let us instead turn, for valuable ideas on art and poetry, to Aristotle's other works, as also suggested by Warry, and as has been already done to some extent by other scholars.

But before we can do that, we must take up the concept of *mimesis*, to which considerable, even disproportionate, attention has been given as a key concept in Aristotle. After this examination, which shall occupy us for awhile owing to the amount of attention given to it, we shall be in a position to move to our main object in this book, and see what Aristotle had to say on organic unity. To dismiss *mimesis* in a paragraph or two would be inadequate, and disappointing to many readers. The reward for this detour will be the removal of the main obstacle to the direct and unimpeded view of what Aristotle had to say on organic unity.

7

A Parenthetical but Unavoidable
Excursus into *Mimesis*

Analysis of the Text

☞ First of all, let us observe that *mimesis*[1] is an instance of
the way Aristotle took over and modified Plato's concepts.[2]
Briefly, that all poetry is *mimesis* is affirmed in *Phaedrus*
248E and in *Republic* 2.373B, etc. Plato oscillates between
mimesis as imitation of persons, i.e., mimicry and acting,
which is condemned in *Republic* 3.393–95, and *mimesis*
as the reproduction of things or of the mental image
(φαντάσματος, *Republic* 10.598B) of a thing, which is also
condemned in *Republic* 10.597E, as a copy at three removes
from reality. This last passage brings in the theory of ideas
as archetypes, which was rejected by Aristotle; the other two
meanings, mimicry and reproduction, are to be found in
him, but as something positive, innocent and even artistic,
and possibly developed and improved, as we shall see.

The preceding paragraph has shown that there are two
meanings of *mimesis* in Plato, if not more. In Aristotle's
Poetics, I believe that at least five meanings are distinguish-
able. Putting together what has been already observed by
students of the *Poetics* and summing it all up, we get these
five meanings of *mimesis* and its cognates (μιμεῖσθαι, etc.):

1) *"Making* something like something else," so that the thing made bears a resemblance to something or to somebody, e.g., a portrait, which is like the person portrayed. We say "so he is like that," and the imitation gives us pleasure (48B6,[3] οἷον ὅτι οὗτος ἐκεῖνος).

2 *"Doing* something like someone else," or imitating his action, e.g., in a play "imitators imitate those who are engaged in action" (48A1, μιμοῦνται οἱ μιμούμενοι πραττοντας). The Greek language distinguished "making" from "doing" (as Romance languages do not). An action is *práxis,* and a making is *poíesis,* from which the meaning "poetry" derives.

3) *Mímesis* is then extended to designate the function of art in general—of all the arts, figurative and plastic, and also dance and music. Chapter 6 brings in the epic and the drama—"each art will admit differences and becomes a different art by imitating with this point of difference, even in dancing, flute-playing, lyre playing," etc. (48A8, ἔσται ἑτέρα τῷ ἑτέρα μιμεῖσθαι τοῦτον τὸν τρόπον, καὶ γὰρ ἐν ὀρχήσει καὶ αὐλήσει καὶ κιθαρίσει). All kinds of poetry are designated as *mímésis* in chapter 1 of the *Poetics.* Differently from the passages from Plato quoted above, it is not stated clearly which meaning of *mímesis* is referred to. But neither of these meanings is subjected by Aristotle to moral condemnation.

4) *Mímesis* may refer to the genre to which a work of literature belongs, as specified by the accompanying adjective; "tragic mímesis" meaning tragedy, "epic mímesis" meaning the epic. Here again *mímesis* is a general term for a work of poetry, without any hint of blame (61B26, πότερον δὲ βελτίων ἢ ἡ ἐποποικὴ μίμησις ἢ ἡ τραγικὴ).

5) Finally it is acknowledged that the object of "imitation" in poetry does not have to be a real object, but only a probable, or even just a possible, depending on the "kind of man" involved (51B8, τῷ ποίῳ τὰ ποῖα). Then "the poet's function is to describe, not the things that have happened, but the things that might happen, according to probability or necessity" (51A36–38, οὐ τὸ τὰ γενόμενα λέχειν, τοῦτο ποιητοῦ ἔρλον ἐστίν, αλλ οἷα ἂν γένοιτο καὶ τὰ δυνατὰ κατὰ τὸ εἰκὸς ἢ τὸ αναγκαῖον).

This throws light on the more laconic formulation of chapter 25: "The poet must necessarily imitate things in one of three ways, either as they were or are, or as they are said or thought to be, or as they ought to be" (60B11). The "ought" here is not ethical, but a way of saying "by necessity." This still leaves *mimesis* within the bounds of the possible and does not extend it to the unreal and the fantastic. The "universality" (καθόλου) called for in such passages as 51B7 and 27, and 55B1, appears on careful scrutiny to be a partial generalization—an ἐπὶ τὸ πολύ, as Aristotle might have said—rather than a genuine universal in the full and proper sense of the word which would make poetry a science. Poetry is said to deal "rather with universals" (51B7), rather and not exclusively or completely. Poetry is also said to be "more philosophical than history" (51B5) in a famous passage to which we shall return, but it is never said to be identical with philosophy, the science of the universal.

As we shall see, some critics seem to believe in this identity, or something like it. But if the aim of poetry were actually to convey a general principle, it would be the critic's job to bring it out and formulate it, then subject it to the appropriate philosophical analysis, and draw the logical conclusion. A tragedy like the *Oedipus* could be then refuted as a faulty piece of reasoning, something like this:

> God is good (philosophical principle involved),
> A good God will not allow a righteous man to suffer unjustly (logical inference),
> ∴ Hence the story of Oedipus is false (QED).

To rebut this hypothetical absurdity is it necessary to rehearse the modern critical view, that the story of *Oedipus* is based on the irrationality and savagery of myth, which a sophisticated and sensitive poet has infused with humane feeling and compassion? Only perhaps to recall again the often neglected principle of the lyrical nature of all poetry, including drama.

But whatever the exact meaning attached to this fifth sense of *mimesis,* it is in direct conflict with meanings one and two, which make *mimesis* refer to a single object. A single object is definitely not a general idea, and a general idea is not a single object (unless we adopt something like Plato's theory of ideas, which Aristotle consistently rejected).

Hence the correct conclusion about the meanings of *mimesis* is that advanced by Wackernagel: the concept of *mimesis* in the *Poetics* is at the time too broad and too narrow, and the *Poetics* tries to remedy this by introducing more and more definitions of poetry, some too broad and some too narrow, but never unifying them into a single, comprehensive concept.[4]

Scrutiny of the Critics

The various and contrasting meanings of *mimesis* have naturally given rise to different general interpretations of the *Poetics,* which I will now consider.

We may perhaps distinguish three main tendencies:

A) The "realistic," which grounds itself basically upon meanings 1 and 2 discussed in the first part of this chapter, making all poetry and all art a portrayal or replica (I will consider "representation" in a moment) of what already exists. This interpretation may be qualified in various ways, but essentially it excludes creation, and its philosophical posture is realism.

B) What I will call the "idealistic" interpretation, favored by critics who find the first interpretation too superficial and expect something more profound from Aristotle. These critics tend to assign to *mimesis* an intellectual, or even metaphysical, function, as the vehicle of a concept or of a general principle. *Mimesis* is defined by these critics as the presentation of the Rule through the Instance, of the Universal through the Particular, of the Ideal through the Real, of the Perfect through the Imperfect. This interpretation brings the *Poetics* into line with Hegelian aesthetics and similar intellectualist theories. But I doubt that it can be grounded upon any of the meanings of *mimesis* that we have found in the *Poetics*; it is barely approximated by the fifth, and goes far beyond it.

Support for this interpretation has been sought in some passages of the *Poetics,* which however are not beyond question. In one of his last chapters, Aristotle takes up what he calls "problems" of poetics, and he returns again (if the text is authentic and correct) to points he has already discussed. He gets into an involved and repetitious discussion of the "impossible" in poetry, which his theory strictly taken does not allow. Here he comes closest perhaps to the idealistic theory: "For the purposes of poetry a convincing impossibility is preferable to an unconvincing possibility; and if men such as Zeuxis depicted be impossible, the answer is that it should be better like that, and the artist ought to improve upon his model" (τὸ γὰρ παράδειγμα δεῖ ὑπερέχειν, 61B13–14).

The characttrs of tragedy are also required to be "better" (βελτιόνων, 54B9) than ordinary men. But this improvement upon the model and upon the average does not lead to a statement of ideal beauty, or of moral perfection as the goal of poetry, as it seems logically required. This interpretation is found in several authoritative critics. Zeller has it: "Art according to Aristotle must represent not the individual as such, but the universal, the necessary and the natural" (2: 305). It is in Butcher: fine art according to Aristotle "discovers the form (εἶδος) towards which an obejct tends, the result which nature strives to attain but rarely or never can attain. Beneath the individual it finds the universal" (pp. 150–154). The "form" (εἶδος) is of course a universal. And so Atkins: "Poetry . . . is the representation of the universal characteristics of human life and thought."[5] McKeon varies it somewhat: "Art does not abstract universal forms as science does, but imitates the forms of individual things."[6] This form however is still an Aristotelian form, i.e., a universal. It does not seem to be an image of the concrete, the individual and particular as such, which is assumed in later aesthetics.

One of the passages of the *Poetics* which is most frequently cited by followers of this interpretation is the famous comparison between poetry and history. Here it is in Bywater's translation: "Hence poetry is something more philosophic and of graver import than history, since its statements are of a nature rather of universals, whereas those of poetry are singulars" (51B5–7). I have already called attention to that "rather" (μᾶλλον) which qualifies the "universal" of poetry. But what Aristotle says here about history is a remarkable example of how far apart the modern view of history is from Aristotle's. For us, history deals with nations, movements, events—all collective entities; for Aristotle, it is nothing more than a series of biographies, the tale of Tom, Dick, and Harry. A very poor idea of history, from our point of view. But history hadn't developed very far in Aristotle's time, and in any case he could not have that consciousness of history which is one of the great achievements of the nineteenth century.[7]

Granting that, we can still afford to smile at A. B. Walkley's parody of that famous passage, which he turned into a definition of the art of the cinema ("moving pictures" in his day): "Picture poetry is a more philosophical and liberal thing than history; for history expresses the particular, picture poetry the not too particular. The particular is, for example, what Alcibiades did or suffered. The not too particular is what Charlie Chaplin did or suffered."[8] The general grounds for this interpretation have also already been discussed in the analysis of *mimesis,* sense 5.

C) What I will call the "Romantic" interpretation, which goes to the length of identifying *mimesis* with the Creative Imagination of Romantic aesthetics.[9] This would have Aristotle anticipate what may be considered one of the highest achievements of later criticism. But, alas, "Aristotle's psychology does not admit of such a faculty as the creative imagination."[10] For him the imagination was merely "weakened sensation" preserved in memory.[11]

D) Lastly, we will discuss "representation" here, which may be considered more an interpretation than a translation of *mimesis,* as is often done. This would avoid the ambiguities of "imitation," and the formula "art is an imitation of reality" becomes "art is a representation of reality," which makes more sense to the modern mind. For to imitate is not the same as to represent, as the German interpreters assume when the translate *mimesis* with *Darstellung,* or *darstellende Abbildung,* or *nachbildende Darstellung,*[12] combining the two terms.

Strictly speaking, in the description of mental processes "representation" means forming a mental picture of something. So when we represent a tree to ourselves, we are not making something like a tree, or doing something like a tree, but making a mental picture which we believe corresponds to the object called a tree. Then by extension "represent" is used for the pictorial portrayal of something drawn from a mental picture, as when we speak of a painting "representing the murder of Abel." To "represent a murder" is not to imitate a murder, which would be to commit another crime. In this extension, art would be a representation.

But Grube has raised this objection: "Aristotle broadens and clarifies the Platonic theory where he later says that, when accused of untruth, the poet may reply that he is imitating things as they are, as they were, or as they ought to be, or as men thought they were, i.e., representing the present, the past, the ideal, or men's beliefs about them. Even so, however, we must still feel the picture to be true to something actual, which is the essence of the theory and the justification of the continued use of the word *mimesis* as imitation; this feeling is lost in the alternative translation as 'representation.' "[13] But this runs into all the ambiguities of *mimesis* that we have been analyzing.

Summing up the above, "representation" is not so much

a translation of *mimesis* as an interpretation of it, but an interpretation which perhaps makes most sense of the fluctuating and vacillating text.[14] Historically, these interpretations spread over a considerable period of time, the *Poetics* having been the subject of a vast literature during close to five centuries. The scholar who today takes up the subject should endeavor to be as concise as possible, but some account, even if summary, must be given of the development of previous criticism. So I will give some general impressions, and not a discussion of every single critic and every single question, which would require volumes.

No other book of criticism has had lavished upon it so much ingenuity and erudition, superficiality and dogmatism, misplaced acumen and shrewd analysis, as the *Poetics*. For the modern world, it was begun by the Italian critics of the Renaissance[15] who rediscovered it and made it more or less a bible of criticism, at the very time when the philosopers and the scientists were turning away from Aristotle. As has been wittily said of the Italian Aristotelian critics, "they found him always right, even when they have translated him wrong."[16] But I must make an exception for the physician G. Fracastoro, an expert on venereal disease, who wrote an agile dialogue, the *Navagero* (1585), which expounds a much better aesthetics than many ponderous tomes.[17]

In the eighteenth century the Germans had an enlightened Aristotelian in Lessing. Later came the German critics who dominated the nineteenth century. With a deeper philosophical understanding and a greater precision, they took a broader historical perspective, due to the great development of all these studies in Germany. But they were liable to make Aristotle more profound than he really was, and they built up elaborate systems of aesthetics which they fathered upon him. They avoided the prescriptive pitfall, and were usually lucid in style. This is particularly true of one who is hardly remembered today: Teichmüller.

In 1867–73 Gustav Teichmüller brought out at Halle his

three volumes of *Aristotelische Forschungen,* two of which are concerned with the *Poetics.* The first is a collection of notes on the text, elucidating difficulties and obscurities, but not expounding it paragraph by paragraph. The second volume (1869) is doctrinal, and a whole system of aesthetics, philosophically argued, is built upon the *Poetics,* point by point. It begins by gathering Aristotle's views on art not only from the *Poetics* but from his other works, notably the *Ethics,* the *Metaphysics* and the logical treatises, and arranging them systematically. The third volume (1873) was dedicated to the history of other Greek philosophical concepts. In the twentieth century the fullest commentary was made by Alfred Gudeman (Berlin, 1934).

The French in the nineteenth century maintained on the whole a balanced view and expounded the *Poetics* with clarity and good sense. They criticized the Germans for their excesses but avoided superficial interpretations. E. Egger's book on Greek criticism is a mine of learning and judgment, and C. Bénard's book on the *Poetics* is sound and perceptive.[18] The English generally eschewed the philosophical flights of the Germans and produced two outstanding editions of the *Poetics.* Butcher's (1894) and Bywater's (1909), both provided with translation and commentary. D. S. Margoliouth's book (1911) of commentary and translation—including a Latin translation of an Arabic text—stands alone, both in approach and in conclusions.[19]

The Italians of the twentieth century, having adopted from the Germans the ways of critical scholarship, rejected the prescriptive approach of their Renaissance predecessors and worked entirely with historical methods. They profited from Benedetto Croce's contributions to criticism, philosophy, and history; he, too, had learnt much from the Germans and was not afraid to profess it, while keeping an open mind on their theories. Hence, among others, the penetrating commentary by Rostagni[20] and, one might add, the idealistic interpretation by Valgimigli[21] who translated the *Poetics* in beautiful Italian style.

Then came the Americans (speaking of native Americans, not of European scholars working in America, who may fall under the preceding categories), whose work is mostly on the same general lines as the English, which has tendency to greater detail. Else's commentary[22] is as full as Gudeman's. At the academic level, the *Poetics* enjoyed a revival of popularity and called forth a number of translations, being included in many freshman courses. This could have brought on a revival of orthodox Aristotelianism, like in the Renaissance; but it seems to have left most freshmen unharmed. So much for the interpreters of *mimesis*.

∴

Summing up our excursus into *mimesis,* we conclude that that much debated concept, when closely examined, exhibits a confusion of different meanings, to which the corruption of the text has contributed, and which lead to different and conflicting general theories.[23] As far as our main goal is concerned, it has turned out to be a blind alley, even if some interesting things came up by the way. But in the analysis of *mimesis* we did not find anything that threw light upon the inner structure of the poem or the work of art, as organic unity does. We will therefore now return to that concept.

8

Organic Unity in
Aristotle

Let us now see if we can find in the *Poetics* anything on organic unity. The most definite statement occurs in chapter 7, on Plot. Plot is only one of the six "parts" of tragedy according to Aristotle, the others being Character, Speech, Thought (of the characters, not of the poet), Spectacle, and Melody. The last two are later set aside as unessential (62A11–13), leaving four essential parts. But the list of six parts seems to be of the kind that Kant described in the *Critique of Pure Reason,* at the beginning of the *Analytic*: when we engage in an inquiry into a subject connected with any faculty, "then, as the occasioning circumstances differ, various concepts stand forth . . . and allow of their being collected with more or less completeness. . . . But when the inquiry is carried on in this mechanical fashion, we can never be sure whether it has been brought to completion. Further, the concepts which we thus discover only as opportunity offers, exhibit no order or systematic unity, but are in the end merely arranged . . . in series according to . . . their contents . . . an arrangement which is anything but systematic, although to a certain extent methodically instituted."[1] This applies exactly to the famous enumeration of the six parts of tragedy. Goethe put it in a nutshell: Aris-

totle's enumertion of the parts of tragedy is like saying that
a man is made up of soul, body, hair, and clothes.[2] Mere
taxonomy, and not very good at that.

However that may be, Aristotle states that plot is the most
important part of tragedy, and discusses it at length, bringing in the organic simile: "to be beautiful, a living creature
[*zóon*] and every whole made up of parts, must not only
present a certain order in the arrangement of parts, but also
be of a certain definite magnitude. Beauty is a matter of
size and order [*táxei*]" (50B38).[3]

He gets still closer to organic unity in his particular description of a good plot: it "must represent one action, a
complete whole, with its several incidents so closely connected that the transposal or withdrawal of any one of them
will disjoin and dislocate the whole" (51A32–35). He has
nothing to say about the double relationship of the parts
and the whole according to Plato: the parts must be in
keeping a) with each other and b) with the whole. So in the
Poetics organicism holds, to a certain degree, only for one
part of the composition, not for the whole.

Let us therefore go outside the *Poetics* to look for statements on organic unity in Aristotle's other works. I shall
not attempt a full analysis, as I have attempted for the
Poetics, but only quote relevant passages from them. Nor
shall I attempt to relate each quotation to the framework
of concepts in which it appears in that work. That would
take us too far out.[4] However, I shall try not to distort or
misinterpret these partial quotations.

Outside the *Poetics,* the following discussions in other
works of Aristotle are relevant to organic unity: 1) the concept of unity, 2) the concept of organism, and 3) the concept
of art. We will take them in order.

1. Unity

Aristotle defines unity in book Delta of the *Metaphysics,*
which is a kind of philosophical dictionary. Here (1015B)
he distinguishes four kinds of unity: 1) unity by continuity,

2) unity by completeness, 3) unity of substance or matter, so that the unit cannot be divided up, and 4) by identity of genus: "isosceles and equilateral triangles are one figure, because they are triangles." These four kinds of unity may perhaps correspond, in a vague way, to Aristotle's famous four causes: efficient, final, material, and formal, as expounded, e.g., in *Metaphysics* 7. 2. 1013A21.

Defining the first kind, unity by continuity, Aristotle says: "Things are essentially continuous when they are one not merely by contact. Thus, if you placed a number of sticks so that they touched one another, you would not on that account describe them as one piece of wood, or one continuum at all" (1015B8–10). The second kind of unity, "completeness," as we have translated it, belongs according to Aristotle especially to living beings (1016A25), so we will postpone our discussion of it until we come to the organic in Aristotle. The third kind, "individuality," refers to the unity of the substance or matter of which a thing is made, so it belongs to the discussion of form and matter, which we shall have later. The fourth kind of unity is the unity of the genus, which in poetry would be the genre, so it is not to be found in a single poem but refers to a number of poems of the same class.

Aristotle has more to say on unity that is relevant to poetry, when he discusses in the same book the idea of "the whole." Here he introduces an important concept, and one that is fundamental to his whole philosophy, namely the concept of Form—we deny that a thing has unity "unless the thing is a genuine whole, that is unless its form has unity." Aristotle here applies it not to a work of art but to an artifact, a shoe. A "scrambled" shoe may have all its parts and they may be connected together, but it does not possess unity because it does not have the form of a shoe (1016B11).

In defining a whole, Aristotle distinguishes between a whole in which the order of the parts is indifferent, which he calls not a whole but an "all," from a whole which has a beginning, a middle, and an end (1024A4), and in which the position of the parts makes a difference. In speaking of the "all," in which the order of the parts is indifferent, W. D. Ross in his commentary on the *Metaphysics*,[5] happily hits upon the term "aggregate," which can be used appropriately in criticism to designate compositions devoid of organic unity without recurring to metaphors drawn from biology. The aesthetic relevance of the concept is also manifested in Aristotle's own terms, for "beginning, middle and end" are required for the unity of the plot in the *Poetics* (50B26).

Now for the question that Aristotle has not asked in the passages quoted so far: is a poem a unit or an aggregate? Aristotle answers that question variously for the greatest of Greek poems, the *Iliad,* but he takes it up repeatedly, which shows that poetry was never far from his mind. The *Iliad* is an aggregate according to *Metaphysics,* book H (1045A13): "A definition [ὅρος] is one formula not by placing together, like the *Iliad,* but by being a formula of one thing." So also apparently in this passage of the *Posterior Analytics* (93B35): "A propostion [*lógos*] may be a unity in two ways, either by conjunction [συνδέσμῳ[6]] like the *Iliad,* or because it exhibits one term . . . as the predicate of another term." But the most positive statement, perhaps, is to be found in *Metaphysics,* book Delta, when Aristotle defines "from" or "out of" and brings together his three basic concepts of unity, form, and purpose (*télos*), referring to the *Iliad*: "to be from the composite of matter and form, as the parts from the whole and the single verse[7] from the *Iliad,* and the stones from the home: for the form is an end, and that which has a form is complete." So even in defining unity, Aristotle brings in his fundamental dyad of Form and Matter.

2. The Organism

The concept of the organism in Aristotle is governed by a factor we have not yet considered, teleology, or the definition of the aim or purpose of something. For Aristotle this factor is more evident in works of nature than in works of

art. As Jaeger put it: "Nature is purposive to a higher degree
than art, and . . . the purposiveness that rules in handiwork,
whether art or craft, is nothing but an imitation of this
purposiveness of nature."[8] Aristotle, too, has never seen
a poem as beautiful, or as purposive, as a tree. Here we may
ask: what is the purpose, or *télos,* of a poem? Aristotle answers that question explicitly for one kind of poem, tragedy,
when he says that the "end" of tragedy is the plot (1450A22).
But, having got so far, Aristotle does not here enumerate
other features common to a poem and a living being.

In his treatise *On the Soul* Aristotle gives a description of
the organism (4126B1). There he says that a living body
possesses instruments to perform its functions and attain
its purpose. "Instruments" in Greek are called *organa*
(ὄργανα) so the body possessing them is described as *orga-
nikón* (ὀργανικόν). Being alive it also possesses a soul *(psyché),*
which Aristotle defines philosophically as the actuality, or
entelechy, of the body, whose finality is in itself. A fuller
definition is given in the *De partibus animalium,* or *On
the Parts of Animals.* (Be it noted incidentally that "parts
of animals" is not identical with what we call organs, but
something more general, e.g., it includes the blood.)[9]

"If man and the animals and their parts are products of
nature, account must be taken of their flesh, bone and blood,
in fact of all their parts . . . ; and it must be explained how
it comes to pass that each of these is characterised as it is, and
by what force it is effected. It is not enough to state simply
the substances out of which they are made. . . . If we were
describing a bed or any like article, we should endeavor to
describe the form of it rather than the matter (bronze or
wood) or, at any rate, the matter if described as belonging
to the concrete whole [σύνολον]. For example, the bed is a
certain form in a certain matter" (640B18–27).

This passage has been singled out as clearly implying the
well-known organic principle that the whole is more than
the sum of the parts.[10] Foreshadowings of this principle may
be found in Plato, when he said that "the all is not the

whole" (*Theaetetus* 204B). In the *Parmenides* comes the distinction between simple and complex unity: the first is indivisible, the second is made up of parts (137C). So again we come in Aristotle to the basic dyad of Form and Matter, this time as the constituents of the organism.

3. Art

Let us now turn to what is for us the heart of the matter: what is art for Aristotle? By "art" we moderns generally mean the fine arts, while for Aristotle the word "art" (*téchne*) stood both for the arts and for the crafts, there being no general term for the latter. For Aristotle's definition of art, in his sense, we do not have to rely solely on the fragment of the *Poetics*; art is defined repeatedly in his other works, like the *Metaphysics,* the *Ethics,* and even the *De partibus animalium.* We could even adapt the saying about England, and ask what do they know of Aristotle's poetics who only the *Poetics* know? The definition of art in the other works, at all events, appears more definite, more profound, and more pregnant of fruitful consequences for literary criticism than any in the *Poetics.*

This definition is: Art is the imposition of a certain form (in the Aristotelian sense) upon a certain matter (also in the Aristotelian sense). E.g., "by matter I mean, for instance, bronze; by form, the figure: the composite of the two is the statute" (*Metaphysics* 1029A3).[11] This makes the dominance of form over matter the fundamental principle of Aristotle's aesthetics, with some additional clarifications which I will now make. For Aristotle there are basically three kinds of mental activity—the "theoretical," dealing with knowledge, the "practical," dealing with actions (*práxeis*) or doing, and the productive (or "poietic") arts, in which an object is produced, or "making." Usually it does not seem of primary interest to Aristotle to specify whether the object produced is a thing of beauty or for practical use. Often when defining art he describes it as the process of "making a house [equals a habitation] or a statue" (*Posterior Analytics* 95A4), as if the object produced were indifferent. According to his general definition of art, medicine is also an art, because it induces the form of health in the matter of the body (*De partibus animalium* 639B18). In the *Nicomachean Ethics* (1140A10 f.) he differentiates sharply between doing and making, and proceeds to define art thus: "Doing is not making, nor making doing. Now as building is an art, and is defined as a capacity [*éxis*] conjoined with reason, which is apt to make houses, so art, in its proper sense, must be a capacity, conjoined with reason [*metà lógon*], apt to make."

Note the role of reason (*lógos*) in the artistic process. There are also passages in which Aristotle points out that form in art is something mental. "From art are produced those things whose form is in the mind" (*Metaphysics* 1032B1: ἀπὸ τέχνης δέ γίγνεται, ὅσων τὸ εἶδος ἐν τῇ ψυχῇ). And no less explicitly in the *De partibus animalium* (639B16): "The physician or the builder sets before himself something quite definite—the one, health, apprehensible by the soul [*psyché*], the other a house, apprehensible by the senses; and once he has got this, each of them can tell the causes and reasons [*lógous*] for everything he does and why it must be done as he does it. For the *lógos* is always the *arché* [beginning or principle] for products of Nature as well as for those of Art [*téchne*]."

But this *lógos* being a general idea designates the *kind* of thing produced, and not the characteristics of the individual object that make it different from all others of the same kind. The only way that Aristotle apparently had of differentiating one statue from another was from the subject, the statue of a god or of a mortal, of a man or a woman, or the portrait of a good man rather than that of a bad man (*Poetics* 48A1–5). We moderns think that Hermes sculptured by Phidias will be different from the one by Praxiteles or by Scopas, and even from another Hermes by the same sculptor. Generalities do not help here; individuality must be the goal of the aesthetic judgment. While Aristotle had a definite idea about the individual in living beings, he had little or no concern about the individual in the work of art. This is the extent of Aristotle's intellectualism. But, I repeat, even the general is not the universal.

What is for us the mental object that the artist or the poet has in mind in the act of creation? This *lógos,* as Aristotle has it, this *eidos,* as he also calls it, this "phantasm" as Plato called it (*Republic* 598B), call it what you will, is the object that will become central in modern aesthetics, which will see in it the quality of beauty, and call the activity directed toward it by a variety of names: imagination, *Phantasie,* intuition, *Anschauung,* invention, creativity, and even (although crookedly) "objective correlative." This activity governs the fashioning of the work, which when completed becomes the object of art appreciation, of criticism, and of art history.

One of the main differences between the ancient and the modern view of art seems to be the ancients were mainly concerned with the relation between an external object and the work of art that presents a likeness to it, be it the figure of a human being or the action in a play or in a novel; and so they usually called it *mimesis,* also usually translated "imitation." As a principle, this became the maxim "Art is the imitation of Nature," which according to Jaeger[12] is first found in Aristotle's fragmentary *Protrepticus,* although Aristotle criticized Alcidamas for saying that the Odyssey is "a mirror of life,"[13] whereas the modern view is more concerned with the relation of the work to what was in the mind of the artist when he produced it, and tends to consider the production of this image or mental nucleus as the fundamental act of creation, regardless of any resemblance of the work to some external object. Indeed that work may well be unlike anything in nature, as we can see in modern art, and yet be perfect insofar as it realizes the artist's conception. This basic shift in point of view from the external to the internal corresponds to the general trend of modern speculation inward rather than outward, or to the subjective rather than the objective. Even Plato's organic unity was a property of the work of art and not of the artist's mind.

Aristotle comes very near the subjective nature of art when, in the treatise *On Memory* 450B32, he observes that a painting can be looked at in two different ways: either as a portrait, say of Coriscus, and then it is a likeness of a person, or as pure contemplation: "different is the feeling of contemplation itself" (ἄλλο τὸ πάθος τῆς θεωρίας ταύτης). But he does not go on to define the nature of this contemplation, and therefore stops short of modern aesthetics, which considers the painting the product of the creative imagination.

As we saw, Aristotle's concept of the imagination was that of a weakened sensation, and so purely passive; but in the book *On the Soul* 434A5–10 he distinguishes merely sensuous imagination, or the weakened sensation, from what he calls "deliberative sensation," which is active, because it compares images and grades them according to standards. He concludes: it follows that what acts in this way must be able to make a unity out of several images (ὥστε δύναται ἕν ἐκ πλειόνον φαντασμάτων ποιεῖν). Now to make a unified image out of previous images or impressions is a synthetic act, approximating the a priori synthesis of Kant. But Aristotle leaves it there and goes no further.

However, in his theory of the state he enunciates the principle that "the whole must be considered prior to the parts." He applies it to the relation between the state and the citizens who compose it (*Politics* 1. 2. 1253A20). That priority has since been extended to the aesthetic principle: the unity of a work of art has been conceived as an a priori, or purely mental, even though the parts so unified are usually drawn from experience, or a posteriori.[14]

So, as all roads lead to Rome, we have seen that all lines of investigation on Aristotle's ideas about art, unity, and the organic, lead back to the basic dyad of Form and Matter (which does not exclude the concomitant final and efficient causes). Now the dyad should apply also to works of literature, which we consider art. But what was literature for

Aristotle? To begin with, he had no term for it; but having
the idea of it, he was aware of this lack: "We have no common name for compositions in verse and dramatic compositions in prose, dialogues, etc." (*Poetics* 47B9–12). However he did not proceed further in this direction, beyond
saying that a good prose style is different from a good poetic
style (*Rhetoric* 1404A25), and concentrated on poetry, especially two kinds, epic and dramatic. Of the lyric as a specific
genre he apparently had no conception, though it looms
large for us, and though the Greeks had produced by his
time some of the greatest lyrical poets of world literature,
such as Sappho and Pindar. Aristotle takes notice only of
some sub-genres of the lyric, the dithyramb and the nome,
because they were accompanied by music, a different art
(*Poetics* 47B26), which makes them a combination of arts.

We moderns are not only very much aware of the lyric
as a genre, but also have produced theories that all poetry is
in essence lyrical, even the narrative and dramatic. Accept-
ing Aristotle's definition of art as Form and Matter, we may
ask: can the lyric, as we understand it, be conceived in terms
of form and matter? This leads to the common distinction
between form and content, which however is not merely a
variant of form and matter. It is to be found before Aristotle, in Plato though not in those terms, but as "arrangement" and "invention" (διάθεσις and εὕρεσις in *Phaedrus*
236A, as noted by Grube).[15]

In literature we usually speak of form and content; but
eventually this distinction can be resolved into the distinction of form and matter derived from Aristotle. For instance, at the lowest level, the most external, which Aristotle himself rejected (*Poetics* 37B2–20), the meter of a
poem is its form and everything else in it can be its content
—words, images, feelings, ideas, themes, motifs, etc. At a
somewhat higher level, the way the thoughts are arranged
in a poem could be considered its form, and the thoughts
themselves, with the words, the sentences, the images, and
anything else that conveys thought, would be its contents,

or if we prefer the Aristotelian term, its matter. Note that in this formulation meter which was considered form in the previous formulation is now downgraded to matter. But it is not un-Aristotelian to consider that objects possessing a form of their own may become the matter of a higher form.

A still more sophisticated criticism would consider the system of images in the poem as its form and everything else as its matter. The system of images would be considered as a single, dynamic unit, which unfolds, develops, rises and sinks, widens and narrows, as the poem proceeds, in a way that is satisfactory to the aesthetic sense and for which no rules can be given. A suitable example would be Coleridge's *Kubla Khan,* which on the surface is little more than a succession of brilliant images, tenuously held together by a thin thread of narrative—the narrative of a vision or dream, which constitutes the maximum of subjectivity. Furthermore, the poem is admittedly incomplete. Yet today it is acknowledged a great poem. The images follow a sequence that develops spontaneously as the poem proceeds, until the mind is filled with a single translucent vision. The words, the meter, the syntactic movements, all are subordinated, and contribute to, this vision, and may be considered the matter of the poem. Yet each of them can be taken out of he poem and considered by itself, and generally traced to some historical antecedent, as was done in the well-known book by J. L. Lowes in 1927 almost, but not quite, to exhaustion—not quite, for this line of research seems to know no end. Yet even Lowes did not claim that this analysis of the matter accounted for the poetry, which is the real form of the poem.

Somewhat similar arguments may be made for various imagist and symbolist poems, even if not for all of them. But what has been done to a lesser degree is to interpret narrative and dramatic poems according to his method; lesser, with the exception of Croce, who formulated the principle and applied it widely as a critic. However, as Croce would remind us, for a full account of the poem the charac-

terization of the image should be united with a characterization of the feeling expressed, since all poetry is ultimately
lyrical. This characterization of feeling is a task that calls
for, not psychological theories, but a fine sense for the
shades of emotion and that skill in sizing up elusive personalities of artists which is an endowment of good critics,
like—in different ways and at different times—Pater and
Croce, L. Strachey and Frank Kermode, and others.

It is not conceivable that the applications of form and
matter outlined above are not the only applications of which
that dyad is capable. But in the *Poetics* that dyad is not mentioned, and lyrical poetry not studied. Gudeman explains
this by noting that "in his time the lyric, apart from the
dithyramb, was completely silent" (p. 81). What Aristotle
did dilate upon was tragedy, corresponding to the high level
it had reached by his time. After defining tragedy, Aristotle
analyzed its parts. But these parts are not the basic two of
form and matter, but that set of six: plot, character,
speeches, thought, music and spectacle. It is hard to see how
to make the dyad of Form and Matter jibe with this list.

To obviate this deficiency, and to bring the *Poetics* in
line with Aristotle's basic conceptions, it has been suggested
by scholars that the element of plot (*muthos*) should be considered the form of tragedy, because Aristotle says that it is
"the most important part and almost the soul of tragedy"
(50A38, ἀρχὴ μὲν καὶ οἷον ψυχὴ ὁ μῦθος τῆς τραγῳδίας), and that it
is the purpose (*télos*) of tragedy (50A42). Now, it is argued,
since for Aristotle the soul was the form of the body (*De
anima,* 402A6), plot must be the form of tragedy. But these
are metaphorical and emphatic expressions, not to be taken
literally, as indicated by the "almost" (οἷον) that Aristotle
inserts before "soul."

A different solution to this question was advanced by
Teichmüller. He made plot not the form, but the matter
of tragedy: and the form is the concept of the tragic, "*das
Tragische*" (2: 68). Like the geometrical properties of the
sphere which do not have to be discovered by the maker

of a bronze sphere, *"das Tragische"* is not something that
has to be discovered by the poet, "sondern dies lässt sich als
eine unvergängliche Form der Handlungen erkenne, und
der Künstler muss nur die Fabeln so bilden, dass sie die
Eigenschaften des Tragischen annahme."[16] That is conceiv-
ably the function of matter, to adapt itself so as to bring out
the properties of its form.[17]

To conclude this discussion, if plot is the form of tragedy,
it would be only one half of an arch over a chasm, a lame
duck without its other leg, matter. This goes to show how
near Aristotle gets to the concept of organic unity without
defining it clearly and fully. But he made a basic contribution to criticism with his dyad of Form and Matter. Since
these two usually imply each other—there is no form without matter, except God, and no matter without form, except
"primary" matter—can organic unity be predicted of the
union of form and matter? To do so, the parts of the union
should be in keeping with each other and with the whole.
Can one say that Aristotle's matter is in keeping with its
form? While so-called "primary" matter is mere potentiality, "secondary" matter consists of already-constituted com-
posites (not aggregates) of form and matter, downgraded to
become matter of a higher form.[18] So whole poems, not to
speak of plots, themes, stories, ideas, can undergo such a
fate, and become what scholarships calls the "sources" of the
poem. The whole will not be a unified composition if these
secondary matters are not in keeping with the higher form
imposed upon them.

Finally, a word about the concept of "organic form,"
which occurs in modern criticism. Presumably, it is a form
organically related to its matter, as defined above. The
concept is useful in drawing attention from the ex-
trinsic and mechanical conception of form to the more in-
trinsic and organic conception. But it does not seem to have
been very clearly defined. This is how a modern critic, who
uses it fruitfully, described it: "The notion of organic form
envisages the work of art as a unique principle of life which

permeates and vitalises external form, or conversely as a form embodying life, identical with and inseparable from it."[19] This idea owes something to Schiller's emphatic statement, "In a truly beautiful work of art, the content should do nothing, the form everything. . . . the real artistic secret . . . consists in . . . annihilating the material by means of the form,"[20] which in turn owes something to Schiller's mentor Kant, who conceived of content as sensuous, and form as thought.

I conclude this chapter noting that Aristotle was not an assertor of organic unity to the same degree as Plato was. These two have been coupled together in this connection by critics. Relying on them, I, too, have done so in previous summary statements on the subject.[21] Having scrutinized the texts, I now correct myself. Plato remains the originator and main formulator of the concept; Aristotle takes a shaky second place in its history.

9

Later Criticism

Longinus

✍ It is a commonplace of scholarship that the work by Longinus entitled *On the Sublime*[1] is not by Longinus and it is not on the sublime, at least as it has been understood since the seventeenth century. Yet it is perhaps the most brilliant literary analysis of antiquity, and rich in references to Plato. It is not by the Longinus known to history[2] but by an anonymous writer, probably of the first century A.D.; and "sublimity" does not exactly render the subject of the book: "fine writing" is perhaps closer. The word "sublime" was used by Milton, among others, and it designates a quality often found in Milton's best passages. By the eighteenth century it came to mean a certain elevation of style, together with a certain elevation of subject.[3]

"Longinus" analyzed fine writing by means of the rhetorical classifications of figures of speech, which is taxonomical, but for every class he provided beautiful examples from literature, and usually added a critical commentary of his own which was as fine as the writing. He is, among other things, the first Western critic to quote the Bible for beauty: the creation of light in *Genesis* 1: 3, a passage which can be considered sublime also in the later sense. In spite of his taxonomic procedure, he resorts to organic unity in his famous passage on Sappho in chapter 10, which has also the merit of having preserved most of that great ode of Sappho's for us. He points out that the quality of the poem is due to the poet's skill in "choosing the most suitable particulars and arranging them so that they form a single living body. The particulars involved are the symptoms of passionate love"; "she selects the chiefest of them and binds them one with the other"; "she summons the spirit, the body, the ears, the tongue, the color," and unites them. He also points out that some of these symptoms are "contradictory, she at once shivers and burns, is insane and sane," etc., thus, we may note, exemplifying once more the Heraclitean principle of the unity of opposites (cf. chapter 40).[4]

Plotinus

Plotinus developed a complete system of philosophy mainly from Plato, hence he is called a Neoplatonist; but he also derived ideas from Aristotle and later thinkers. To what exact degree, and in what precise manner, Plato and Aristotle and the post-Aristotelian schools of Skepticism and Stoicism contributed to the system of Plotinus, is a question to which different answers have been offered, and we shall not go into it, but will take up the system as presented in Plotinus. He did not expound it systematically in a single work, but left a large number of separate discussions of particular points, which he refers to his general principles. These separate discussions, to the number of fifty-four, were collected by his devoted disciple Porphyry and arranged in sets of nine, entitled *Enneads* or "groups of nine." So there is no gradual, step-by-step exposition of the whole doctrine. As Mackenna, the translator, warned, "the entire system is assumed in each of the separate treatises,"[5] or "*omnia in omnibus.*"

When pieced together, this doctrine assumes a definitely

mystical turn, centering on the concept of the Divinity as "a graded Triad." This triad consists of 1) the undefinable One, 2) "the Intellectual Principle, and [3] the All Soul" (ibid.). The One is the ineffable center from which all else derives by emanation, and to which they all seek to return and merge their indentity in. The Intellectual Principle or *Nous* is the site of the Platonic ideas, such as the good, the just and the beautiful. These three are all recognized by Plotinus: for he is philosophically enough of a Greek to preserve the cult of Beauty.

He began[6] with an eloquent essay on beauty which rings with the enthusiasm of Diotima in the *Symposium,* and which has inspired many later thinkers, especially in the Renaissance. It has been noted that in this essay (1.6) Plotinus rejects "the customary, purely phenomenal definition of beauty as a harmonious proportion of parts in relation to the whole and to each other, combined with agreeable color,"[7] or essentially what we call organic unity. His reasons for this rejection are that, if so, "only a compound could be beautiful," whereas we consider also simple things beautiful, such as "color," "the light of the sun," "gold," "lightning in the night, and the stars," and even single sounds (*Ennead* 1.6.2). He goes on to account for this beauty in things "by communion with the ideal Form," or the Platonist idea of the beautiful, which descends from above on the person or things that exhibit beauty.

But the result of this influence is that the idea "has grouped and coordinated what from a diversity of parts has become a unity . . . it has made the sum one harmonious whole: for the Idea is unity," which is a return to organic unity, thus combining the ideal theory with the organic unity theory.

In a later treatise, usually entitled "On Intellectual Beauty" (5.8), Plotinus takes up the question of the definition of art, and gives an Aristotelian answer: art consists in the imposition of a certain form on a certain matter, the standard example being that of the shapeless block of

marble which becomes a beautiful statue by the imposition
of a certain form. We have here an early stage in the distinction, developed later by German aestheticians, between
aesthetics as the science of the beautiful and aesthetics as
the science of art; the first, of Platonic descent, is able to see
beauty in Nature and persons, the second sees beauty only
in art and in works of art, beauty in nature being a projec-
tion of the imagination of the seer. The first is objective, the
second subjective. Plotinus has something of both.

But Plotinus did not limit himself to generalities about
beauty; he made a specific and acute observation on the art
of tragedy. "Imagine that someone were to criticise a tragedy
for the simple fact that not all its characters are heroes, but
that there are also slaves and some who rudely come out with
gross language. But the tragedy would not be so beautiful,
if one eliminated from it all these inferior characters, because she attains fulness also by means of such characters"
(*Ennead* 3.2.11).

Plotinus indeed understood tragedy better than French
neoclassical critics of the seventeenth and eighteenth centuries. Here we might say that the unity achieved by a work
of art is not only a unity of parts, but also of opposites,
conformably to the Heraclitean concept that Greek philosophy never forgot. It may also be conjectured that Plotinus
was answering Aristotle's maxim that "beauty consists of
size and order" (*Poetics* 50B37) when he said that "Beauty
cannot be made to depend on magnitude" since both large
things and small things can receive beauty from above
(*Ennead* 5.8.2).

The later Platonists, deriving both from Plato and Aristotle, adopt and develop Aristotle's distinctions of unity.
Earlier still, Clement of Alexandria, who was something
of a Platonist, adopted the distinction between simple and
complex unity, or the unity of parts: the former is the one,
the latter the one in many.[8]

But in the Neoplatonists what were previously purely
logical distinctions tend to become real entities: the one
ceases to be simply the principle of unity and becomes the

ultimate reality, the supreme entity of which no description is adequate. Proclus made use of the Aristotelian doctrine of the priority of the whole to the parts to postulate "a certain kind of wholeness [*holótes*] which is prior to the sum of parts, and which does not passively receive this sum, but is wholeness in itself; from it emanates the wholeness consisting of parts."[9] In his *Platonic Theology* he adds to the concept of this apriority the following corollary: "what is in keeping with the One must preexist to the things which split up into a thousand pluralities."[10] These passages of Proclus might be extended to artistic unity, but the extension is not made explicitly.

We cannot leave this period without reference to the critic who apparently levelled a deadly blow to the theory of imitation, and that was Philostratos of Tarsus (ca. 172–245). In his *Life of Apollonius* there is an inquiry as to what makes the presentation of the gods in Greek art more beautiful than the Egyptians': were the Greeks better acquainted with the gods, or was there some other influence at work? Apollonius replies that the Greeks had been guided by something full of wisdom and other than imitation: the imagination [φαντασία], a faculty, he added, more skilled than imitation; "for whereas imitation [*mimesis*] could only fashion what it had seen, imagination could take the unseen as its subject." To this Atkins observes: "Thus was the notion of the creative imagination expounded once and for all; though many centuries were to elapse before its true significance was realised, owing doubtless to the vogue of the Aristotelian term 'imitation.' In the course of time appeared . . . the more ample treatment" provided by the transcendental philosophy, and in England by Coleridge; "but that antiquity was not wholly devoid of some glimpses of the truth is shown at least by this famous definition by Philostratos."[11] So the thesis that the "decline of mímesis" did not occur until "eighteenth-century England"[12] needs to be qualified.

However, there is a snag. The words which conclude the definition of the imagination in Philostratos point in another direction: πρὸς τὴν ἀναφορὰν τοῦ ὄντος, which seems to mean "according to the reference of the real," and on these words there has been a somewhat confused debate. Croce in his history of aesthetics says: "Several historians of aesthetics attach special importance to some passages of the *Life of Apollonius* by Philostratos senior, in which they think they can see the correction of *mimesis* and the first critical statement of the *imaginative creation*. But the imagination which is the subject of this passage of Philostratos is not something different from the Aristotelian *mimesis*, which, as we saw, concerned not only real things, but also, and principally, the possible."[13]

In Latin criticism the organic simile opens the *Art of Poetry* by Horace (vv. 1–9) and echoes of it are heard again (vv. 23 and 32–34). Cicero clearly affirms the unity of form and content, of thought and expression: "Nam cum omnis ex re atque verbis constet oratio, neque verba sedem habere possunt si rem subtraxeris, neque res lumen si verba removeris" (*De oratore* 3.19 ff.).

The influence of these two great writers is felt in the succeeding centuries, in rhetoricians and grammarians, and I shall not attempt to follow it in detail. Also, organic similes to ethical precepts are not rare in the Gospels and in early Christian literature. The philosophical concept of unity, as discussed by Aristotle in his *Metaphysics*, naturally receives careful attention from the Scholastics. Aquinas scrutinizes unity in general in his discussion of the Unity of God, *Summa*, Qu. 3, Art. 7: "Respondeo: V," and Qu. 11, Art. 1, where he repeatedly quotes Dionysius on unity in general.

After all this, it does not come as a surprise to find the organic concept of poetic unity clearly expounded by the greatest of the medieval poet-philosophers, Dante. "Quella cosa dice l'uomo essere bella, cui le parti debitamente si rispondono, per che della loro armonia resulta piacimento. Onde pare l'uomo essere bello, quando le sue membra debitamente si rispondono; e dicemo bello lo canto, quando le voci de quello, secondo debito de l'arte, sono intra sè rispondenti."[14] The only clause needed to complete the definition is the double correlation of parts to the whole and of parts to each other.

When the concept of organic unity in art is traced philosophically to its ultimate principles, it is seen to involve the concept of the synthetic activity of the mind—the mind of the artist that brings together the parts of the work and makes an indissoluble unity out of them. This concept is not entirely alien to the earliest formulations of organic unity. As we noted, there is a subjective trend which occasionally appears even in Plato. In a well-known passage of the *Theaetetus* (184B ff.; cf. *Cratylus* 404B3–4), there is a clear enunciation of the activity of the mind in bringing together the data of different senses. It has been noted that this is a "synthetic activity"[15] and *that* is a Kantian term. For the concept of the synthetic activity of mind was fully developed by Kant, who not only recognized the mental unification of data from different senses, but also the unifying of data from a single sense, thus making all sense knowledge synthetic.[16] This in turn leads to the theory of the transcendental activity of the *I think,* which became *Geist,* the central concept of post-Kantian idealism. The next step after that for literary criticism is to recognize an aesthetic value in the product of mental activity beside the cognitive value. This recognition was made in Kant's *Critique of Judgment,* and was followed up variously in later aesthetic speculation, reaching its clearest formulation in Croce's aesthetics, where it joins the tradition stemming from Vico that conceives cognition of the particular as the essence of aesthetic activity.[17]

To follow the concept of organic unity into all its appearances in modern poetics would be practically to rewrite the history of modern criticism, which I am not attempting. I shall only mention a few scattered but significant references in modern thinkers. One of the earliest thinkers to assert clearly the opposition between the organic and the mechanical was Leibniz, in this limpid statement: "L'unité d'un horloge est tout autre chez moi que celle d'un animal:

celui-ci pouvant être une substance douée d'une veritable
unité . . . même que l'horologe n'est autre chose qu'une
assemblâge."[18] Nor could the idea be absent in Goethe; e.g.:
"In every living being what we call parts are so inseparable
from the whole, that they can be conceived only in it and
with it; neither the parts can serve as measure of the whole,
nor it of the parts."[19]

During the Romantic period organic unity was repeatedly and firmly asserted in English criticism. Coleridge
in 1814 gave this definition of organic unity without there
using the terms. "The sense of beauty subsists in the simul-
taneous intuition of the relation of parts, each to each, and
of all to the whole."[20]

Still earlier, in 1811, in his famous "Lecture" on Shakespeare he had enthusiastically adopted August Schegel's
defence of organic form in Shakespeare: his plays were not
formless, as the neoclassicists claimed, because they did
not follow traditional structure, for they possessed a form
of their own, suited to their matter. "The true ground of
the mistake, as has been well remarked by a Continental
critic,[21] lies in the confounding mechanical regularity with
organic form. The form is mechanic when on any given
material we impress a predetermined form not arising out
of the properties of the material, as when to a mass of wet
clay we give whatever shape we wish it to retain when
hardened. The organic form, on the other hand, is innate; it
shapes as it developed itself from within, and the fulness of
its development is one and the same with the perfection of
its outward form. Such is life, such is the form."[22]

This is only a brief look at the wealth of developments,
applications, and variations of organic unity in later times.
By itself alone it provides only the beginning of a rounded
conception of poetry and of art, necessary but not sufficient
to it. But it is susceptible of considerable extensions, even in
contemporary criticism, where its origins are considered
by only a few investigators in the history of criticism, such
as Erwin Panofsky, Sir Herbert Read, and René Wellek.

Notes
Selected Bibliography
Index

Notes

1. Prelude: The Antinomies of Criticism

1. Suggested by B. Croce's "Le antinomie della critica d'arte" (1906), in *problemi di estetica* (1910; 4th ed., Bari, 1949), pp. 42–45. Ultimately by Kant's "Antinomy of Taste" and "Its Solution," *Critique of Judgment,* nos. 56–57; not to speak of the "Second Antinomy of Pure Reason," *Critique of Pure Reason,* A434, B462.

2. Or what is called "immanent poetics" by M. Wojeck, "Symbol, Organic Unity and Modern Aesthetic Subjectivism," *Zeitschrift für Anglistik und Amerikanistik* 18 (1970): 355 ff.

3. J. Gadol, *Leon Battista Alberti, Universal Man of the Early Renaissance* (Chicago, 1969), p. 121. We shall have occasion to discuss this supposed fragment of Philolaos in the next chapter.

2. The Pre-Socratic Preparation

1. See G. M. A. Grube, *The Greek and Roman Critics* (London, 1965), pp. 1–15. For a more detailed account (largely inferential) see E. Della Valle, *Lezioni di poetica classica,* 2 vols. (Naples, 1945–46).

2. W. K. C. Guthrie, *A History of Greek Philosophy,* 3 vols. (Cambridge, 1967–69), translates it "the Boundless" (1: 83).

3. On its earlier history see R. Padellaro, *Il problema cosmologico e l'antinomia Uno-Molteplice nei Presocratici,* Publicazioni dell'Istituto di Filosofia della Università di Genova, N. 23 (Milan, 1962). See also S. Caramella, "Unità," in *Enciclopedia filosofica* (Venice, 1937), 4: 1395–1406, and A. Diès, "Le Problème de l'Un et du Multiple avant Platon," *Revue d'histoire de la philosophie* 1 (1927): 5–22.

4. *The Decline and Fall of the Roman Empire* (1781), ed. W. Smith, 8 vols. (1854; new impression, London, 1908), 3: 45–46.

5. "Plato," in *Representative Men* (1850; reprint ed., London, 1926), pp. 211–14.

6. *Pragmatism* (1907; reprint ed., New York, 1956), p. 90.

7. F. M. Cornford, *Plato's Theory of Knowledge* (London, 1933), p. 151.

8. B. Bosanquet, *History of Aesthetic* (2d ed., 1904; reprint ed., New York, 1957), p. 30.

9. On this point, and for other discussions of this passage, see D. Pesce, *Idea, numero ed anima: Primi contributi a una storia del neoplatonismo nell'antichità* (Padua, 1961), pp. 61 ff.

10. G. W. F. Hegel, *Lezioni sulla storia della filosofia*, trans. G. Sanna and E. Codignola (Florence, 1930), 1: 239–40.

11. See now fully W. Tatarkiewicz, *History of Aesthetics,* ed. J. Harrell, 3 vols. (The Hauge, 1970), 1: 80 ff.

12. "The word *harmonia,* a key-word of Pythagoreanism, meant primarily the joining or fitting of things together, even with the material peg with which they were joined" (Guthrie, *A History of Greek Philosophy,* 1: 220*n*). See also the references to "harmony" in K. Freeman, *The Pre-Socratic Philosophers: A Companion to Diels, "Fragmente der Vorsokratiker"* (Cambridge, Mass. and Oxford, 1946), pp. 113–14, 119–20, 122–24, 183–85, 222–24, 230–31, 254–55, 384*n*.

13. *Nicomachean Ethics* 1106B14.

14. This is a commonplace of history. See it ably restated by Guthrie, *A History of Greek Philosophy,* 1: 205 and Tatarkiewicz, *History of Aesthetics,* 1: 85.

15. O. Gilbert, "Aristoteles Urteil Über die Pythagorische Lehre," *Archiv für Geschichte der Philosophie* 22 (1890): 28–48, 145–65.

16. E. Zeller, *Outlines of the History of Greek Philosophy,* ed. W. Nestle, trans. L. R. Palmer (1931; reprint ed., New York, 1955), p. 51. See also E. Zeller, *La filosofia dei Greci nel suo sviluppo storico,* trans. R. Mondolfo (Florence, 1932), pt. 1, vol. 2, pp. 444–53. But see H. Cherniss, *Aristotle's Critique of Presocratic Philosophy* (Baltimore, 1935), pp. 390–91.

17. L. L. Whyte, ed., *Aspects of Form: A Symposium on Form in Nature and Art* (1951; reprint ed., Bloomington, Ind., 1961), p. 230.

18. The connection between "Form and Matter" and "Form and Content" requires further elucidation which cannot be given here. Cf. E. K. Mundt, "Three Aspects of German Aesthetic Theory," *Journal of Aesthetics and Art Criticism* 17 (1959): 288–89.

19. A beautifully simple demonstration of this inseparability as taught at Oxford will be found in L. P. Smith, *Unforgotten Years* (Boston, 1939), pp. 177–78.

20. *Rhetoric* 1407B11.

21. Guthrie, *A History of Greek Philosophy,* 1: 407–8.

22. Ibid., 450.

23. Ibid., 440.

24. Ibid., 446.

25. *American Heritage Dictionary.*

26. Aristotle (pseud.) *De Mundo* 396B10 (Loeb Classical Library, Cambridge, Mass., 1955), p. 379.

3. Early Literary Criticism

1. Parmenides fgs. 7, 8; K. Freeman, *Ancilla to the Pre-Socratic Philosophers: A Complete Translation of the Fragments in Diels, "Fragmente der Vorsokratiker"* (Cambridge, Mass., 1948), p. 43.

2. Fgs. 7, 8.

3. Fg. 18; Freeman, *Ancilla to the Pre-Socratic Philosophers*, p. 97.

4. B. Croce, *Estetica come scienza dell'espressione e Linguistica Generale: Teoria e Storia* (1902; 9th ed. Bari, 1950), p. 75, condensed.

5. E.g., *Phaedrus* 266B, 277B

6. E. Caird, *Evolution of Religion*, 2d ed. (Glasgow, 1894), p. 150.

7. *Letture di poeti riflessioni sulla teoria e la critica della poesia* (Bari, 1959), p. 235.

8. Quoted by B. Croce, *Poeti e scrittori del pieno e del tardo Rinascimento*, 3 vols. (Bari, 1945), 2: 262.

9. Xenophon *Memorabilia* 1. 5. 11.

10. T. Carlyle, *Life of Sterling* (London, 1871), p. 48. Cf. "On the Philosophic Import of the Words, Object and Subject," in Coleridge's *Complete Works*, ed. W. G. T. Shedd, 7 vols. (New York, 1884), 4: 411–14 especially.

11. R. Pfeiffer, *History of Classical Scholarship, from the Beginnings to the End of the Hellenistic Age* (Oxford, 1969), p. 38.

12. Croce, *Estetica*, p. 77.

13. See my essay in G. S. Rousseau, ed., *Organic Form: The Life of an Idea* (London, 1972), p. 19.

14. G. Vlastos, ed., *The Philosophy of Socrates* (New York, 1971), pp. 1–2. For translations of relevant texts, see Plato and Xenophon, *Socratic Discourses*, with introduction by A. D. Lindsay, Everyman's Library (London, 1910), and Richard Levin, ed., *The Question of Socrates* (New York, 1951).

15. Such as Aristotle, for whom see A. R. Lacey, "Our Knowledge of Socrates," in Vlastos, *The Philosophy of Socrates*, pp. 44–49.

16. It is now considered likely that Xenophon was acquainted with the writings of Plato (Guthrie, *A History of Greek Philosophy*, 3: 342, 347).

4. Plato

1. R. Hackforth, *Plato's Examination of Pleasure* (New York, 1945), pp. 19–20.

2. Cornford, *Plato's Theory of Knowledge*, p. 217.

3. W. Wallace, *Prolegomena to the Study of Hegel's Philosophy and Especially of His Logic*, 2d ed. (Oxford, 1894), p. 344.

4. E. Zeller, *Plato and the Older Academy*, trans. S. F. Alleyne and A. Goodwin (London, 1876), pp. 505–6.

5. The following analysis of the *Phaedrus* develops my previous discussion of it in my "The Ancient Roots of a Modern Idea," in Rousseau, ed., *Organic Form*, pp. 7–23.

6. This is obviously homosexual love, not unusual among the Greeks; but the arguments advanced are so general that they can apply to normal love. As Taylor put it, "for a modern parallel to the paradox we might imagine a clever essay written to show that Tom Jones' conduct toward Lady Bollaston is morally more innocent than his affair with Molly Seagrim" (A. E. Taylor, *Plato: The Man and His Work* [1926; reprint ed., New York, 1956], p. 302).

7. Cf. T. Nashe, *Works,* ed. R. B. McKerrow (Oxford, 1958), 4: 389.

8. Plato, *Phaedrus,* ed. R. Hackforth (Cambridge, 1952; reprint ed; New York, n.d.), pp. 16–18.

9. Grube, *The Greek and Roman Critics,* p. 57n.

10. Attributed to a Cleobulos of Lindos by P. Vicaire, *Platon, critique littéraire* (Paris, 1960), p. 287.

11. *Gorgias* 503E which we shall see later. For "order, harmony and writing" in Plato see Vicaire, *Platon, critique littéraire,* pp. 359 ff.

12. *Phaedrus,* ed. L. Robin (Paris, 1923), p. 70.

13. *Hippias Major* 290 D–E.

14. 266–67, translation adapted from Jowett's and from Hackforth's.

15. "For the understanding of the following argument, it is essential to grasp that the theory (which here is criticised) is materialistic, in the sense that the only 'things' it recognised as the objects of any sort of cognition are concrete individual things, and the perceptible parts of which such things are aggregates" (Cornford, *Plato's Theory of Knowledge,* p. 146). But cf. "the whole is prior to the part" (Aristotle *Politics* 1. 2).

16. So the theory that the whole is greater than the sum of the parts is some two thousand years older than the nineteenth century to which D. C. Phillips would confine it in his paper "Organicism in the late Nineteenth and Early Twentieth Centuries," *Journal of the History of Ideas* 31 (1970): 413–32. It goes back to the Platonic-Aristotelian tradition, and assumes different presuppositions in each of the thinkers that formulate it, the five-point theory that Phillips formulates as the doctrine of "organicism" is a modern construction which ignores history. Cf. C. Mazzantini, "Tutto," in *Enciclopedia filosofica* (Rome, 1957), 4: 134–35.

17. As noted by Cornford, *Plato's Theory of Knowledge,* p. 151, n. 1.

18. Aristotle, *Metaphysics,* trans. H. G. Apostle (Bloomington, Ind., 1966), p. 135 and n. 13.

19. *Phaedrus,* ed. Hackforth, p. 57.

20. On the Greek expressions for beauty, the beautiful, the beautiful and other general terms see also the note in Plato, *Dialogues,* trans. B. Jowett, 4th ed., 4 vols. (Oxford, 1953), 1: 563–64.

21. *Phaedo* 65D, 75D, 78D; *Euthydemus* 500E; *Cratylus* 439C; *Laws* 2. 655C.

22. αὐτὸ τὸ καλὸν ἰδεῖν, εἰλικρινές, καθαρὸν, ἄμεικτον.

23. E. Panofsky, *Idea: A Concept in Art Theory,* trans. J. J. S. Peake (Columbia, S.C., 1968), p. 13.

24. On this important question, amply discussed in the literature on Plato, see Taylor, *Plato,* pp. 388–89.

25. H. A. Wolfson, *Religious Philosophy: A Group of Essays,* (New York, 1965), pp. 27–68.

26. C. Renouvier, *Les Dilemmes de la metaphysique,* 2d ed. (Paris, 1927), p. 27.

27. L. Robin, *Platon: Le Banquet* (Paris, 1929), pp. 69–70.

28. J. I. Beare, *Greek Theories of Elementary Cognition* (Oxford, 1906), p. 261.

29. Cornford, *Plato's Theory of Knowledge,* pp. 105–6.

5. A Cursory Glance at the Scholarship on *Phaedrus* 264C

1. Schleiermacher, *Introductions to the Dialogues of Plato*, trans. W. Dobson (Cambridge and London, 1836), p. 49.

2. G. W. F. Hegel, *The Philosophy of Fine Art*, trans. F. P. B. Osmaston (London, 1920), 1: vi, n. 2.

3. *Die Idee und das Ideal*, nach der erhaltenen Quellen neu herausgegeben von G. Lasson (Hegel, *Sämtl. Werke*, Bd. X a, Vorlesungen über die Ästhetik ler Halbbrand, Philosophische Bibliothek, 164 [Leipzig, 1931]).

4. Hegel, *Lezioni sulla storia della filosofia*.

5. E. Müller, *Geschichte der Theorie der Kunst by der Alten*, 2 vols. (Breslau, 1834–37).

6. *The Phaedrus of Plato*, with English notes and dissertations by W. H. Thompson (London, 1868).

7. I.e., Aristotle *Poetics* 23. 1, and a second century commentary on *Phaedrus*.

8. G. Gentile, "Edoardo Zeller," in *La Riforma della dialettica Hegeliana* (Messina, 1913), pp. 211–17.

9. L. Stefanini, *Platone*, 2d., 2 vols. (Padua, 1949), 1: lxiv–xvi.

10. *Enzyklopädie und Methodologie der klassischen Philogie* (Leipzig, 1877), p. 133.

11. 3d. ed. (Madrid, 1909), 1: 31.

12. C. Bénard, *L'esthétique d'Aristote* (Paris, 1887), p. 25.

13. A. E. Chaignet, *La Rhétorique et son histoire* (Paris, 1888). I do not find a reference to this idea in his previous books on Plato, *La Psychologie de Platon* (Paris, 1862), or *Vie et écrits de Platon* (Paris, 1871).

14. J. Walter, *Die Geschichte der Asthetik im Ältertum, ihrer begrifflichen Entwicklung nach, dargestellt* (Leipzig, 1893), p. 278.

15. Reprinted in *Harvard Lectures on Greek Subjects* (London, 1906).

16. G. Saintsbury, *History of Criticism and Literary Taste in Europe* (London, 1900; reprint ed., New York, 1950), 1: 20–21.

17. T. Gomperz, *Pensatori Greci: storia della filosofia antica*, trans. L. Bandini (Florence, 1944), vol. 3, pt. 1, 161n.

18. J. E. Sandys, *A History of Classical Scholarship* (New York, 1958), 1: 61.

19. Bosanquet, *History of Aesthetic*, pp. 55, 32.

20. Croce, *Estetica*, pp. 172–73, 178.

21. U. von Wilamowitz-Moellendorf, *Platon*, 2d ed. (Berlin, 1920), 1: 481, n. 1.

22. *The Greek View of Poetry* (London, 1931).

23. P. Friedländer, *Platon* (1928, 2d ed., Berlin, 1960), 3: 217–18.

24. W. R. Roberts, *Greek Rhetoric and Literary Criticism* (London, 1928; reprint ed., New York, 1963), p. 7.

25. W. Jaeger, *Paideia: The Ideals of Greek Culture*, trans. G. Highet (New York, 1944), 3: 189.

26. 2d ed., 2 vols. (Padua, 1949). The first edition goes back to 1932, and the later edition is notably augmented. For a shorter exposition, see L. Stefanini, "Platone," in U. A. Padovani, ed., *Grande Antologia Filosofica* (Milan, 1954), 1: 223–321, esp. pp. 227–32.

27. Cherniss, *Aristotle's Critique of Presocratic Philosophy*, p. 11.

28. Stefanini, *Platone*, 2: 11, 19, 21*n.*, 24, 29, 31, 33.

29. Ibid., pp. 35–59.

30. J. W. H. Atkins, *Literary Criticism in Antiquity: A Sketch of Its Development* (London, 1934, rpt. 1952), 1: 54–55.

31. K. E. Gilbert and H. K. Kuhn, *A History of Aesthetics*, rev. ed. (Bloomington, Ind., 1953).

32. J. G. Warry, *Greek Aesthetic Theory: A Study of Aesthetic and Callistic Concepts in the Works of Plato and Aristotle* (London, 1962).

33. Taylor, *Plato*, p. 312.

34. G. M. A. Grube, *Plato's Thought* (1935; reprint ed., Boston, 1958), p. 212.

35. *Phaedrus*, ed. Hackforth, p. 130. In a previous essay, "The Ancient Roots of a Modern Idea," in Rousseau, ed., *Organic Form*, p. 22, n. 10, I credited Professor Hackforth with good intentions, and did not analyze his comments too closely.

36. P. Vicaire, *Platon, critique littéraire*, pp. 359–60.

37. Tatarkiewicz, *History of Aesthetics*, 1: 123.

38. E. Grassi, *Theorie der Schönen in der Antike* (Berlin, 1962), and J. Kruger, *Aesthetik der Antike, Sammlung der Texte* (Berlin, 1964).

6. Aristotle

1. Cf. M. Manquat, *Aristote Naturaliste* (Paris, 1932), and H. D. Kantz, *The Biological Motivation of Aristotle* (New York, 1939).

2. E. Panofsky, *Idea: Ein Beitrag zur Begriffsgeschichte der ältere Kunsttheorie* (Leipzig, 1924), p. 9. I have slightly modified the translation by J. J. S. Peake, p. 17.

3. Aristotle, *On the Art of Poetry*, trans. I. Bywater, with a Preface by G. Murray (Oxford, 1920), pp. 6–8.

4. On this point (as well as for other illuminating points) see F. Solmsen, *Ursprung und Methoden der Aristotelischen Poetik*, (Darmstadt, 1968), pp. 6–10.

5. E. Zeller, *Aristotle and the Earlier Peripatetics*, English translation (London, 1897), 1: 103*n.*

6. Aristotle, *Art of Poetry*, trans. Bywater, p. 4.

7. J. G. Warry, *Greek Aesthetic Theory*, p. 83.

8. "Long before this [i.e., Lessing], in 1786, Warton had compared the *Poetics* to Euclid" (L. Cooper, *The Poetics of Aristotle: Its Meaning and Its Influence* [1923; reprint ed., Ithaca, N.Y., 1956], p. 140).

7. A Parenthetical but Unavoidable Excursus into *Mimesis*

1. For *mimesis* in Greek before Plato, see H. Koller, *Die Mimesis in der Antike. Nachahmung, Darstellung, Ausdruck* (Bonn, 1954); G. Sörböm, *Mimesis and Art: Studies in the Origin and Development of an Aesthetic Vocabulary* (Uppsala, 1966); and D. W. Lucas, "Mimesis," in *Aristotle's Poetics* (Oxford, 1968), pp. 258–72.

2. That Aristotle derived much of his *Poetics* from Plato was the thesis of G. Finsler, *Platon und die Aristotelische Poetik* (Leipzig, 1900), qualified by later scholars. Cf. also E. Bignami, *La Poetica di Aristotele e il concetto dell'arte presso gli antichi* (Florence, 1932). For *mimesis* in Plato, see W. J. Verdenius, "Plato's Doctrine of Artistic Imitation," in G. Vlastos, ed., *Plato: Ethics, Politics and Philosophy*, Modern Studies in Philosophy, vol. 2 (New York, 1971), pp. 259–73.

3. In the references which follow I have for the sake of brevity omitted the first two figures of the number of the page of the *Poetics*, which is always 14; e.g. 48B6 here stands for 1448B6. The translation is basically Bywater's, with some modifications.

4. W. Wackernagel, *Poetik, Rhetorik und Stylistik* (Halle, 1873), pp. 16–17.

5. Atkins, *Literary Criticism in Antiquity*, 1: 103.

6. R. McKeon, "Literary Criticism and the Concept of Imitation in Antiquity" (1936), in R. S. Crane, ed., *Critics and Criticism: Ancient and Modern* (Chicago, 1952), p. 162.

7. Cf. R. Weil, *Aristote et l'histoire: Essai sur la "Politique"* (Paris, 1960).

8. A. B. Walkley, *Pastiche and Prejudice* (London, 1921), p. 11.

9. E. Egger, *Essai sur l'histoire de la critique chez les Grecs* (Paris, 1887) translates *poíesis* by "création" (p. 233) and speaks of art "créatrice" (p. 232), "création raisonnée" (p. 234), and "la création poétique" (p. 235). M. Valgimigli declares that "la mimèsi è una vera e propria attività creatrice dello spirito" in his Aristotele, *Poetica*, 3d ed. (Bari, 1946), p. 36.

10. Aristotle, *Poetics*, trans. S. H. Butcher (New York, 1907), p. 126.

11. For a fuller discussion of Aristotle's views on imagination see W. M. Bundy, *The Theory of the Imagination in Classical and Medieval Thought* (Urbana, Ill., 1927), p. 75.

12. A. Gudeman, Aristoteles, περὶ ποιητικῆς, (Berlin, 1934), p. 80.

13. Grube, *The Greek and Roman Critics*, p. 71.

14. "Representation" as a translation of *mimesis* has been defended particularly by F. M. Cornford. *The Republic of Plato*, (Oxford, 1941), p. 323.

15. They are the subject of a minute analytical study by B. Weinberg, *A History of Literary Criticism in the Italian Renaissance*, 2 vols. (Chicago, 1961). Considerable research on individual critics has been done since, both in Italy and elsewhere. For earlier views on them, see J. E. Spingarn, *La critica letteraria nel rinascimento* (Bari, 1905), which contains more than the English edition of 1899, and V. Hall, *Renaissance Literary Criticism: A Study of Its Social Content* (New York, 1945). Croce's contributions will be dealt with in the next note.

16. F. L. Lucas, *Studies in French and English* (London, 1934), p. 303. For historical considerations that qualify the above judgment, see B. Croce's *Estetica*, pt. 2, ch. 2; his *Problemi di estetica*, pp. 452–53; *Nuovi saggi di estetica*, 2d ed. (1926), pp. 98–99; *Conversazioni critiche* (1932), 3: 36–39; *Poeti e scrittori del . . . Rinascimento*, 2: 85–86, 142; *Poesia popolare e poesia d'arte* (1933), pp. 350–52. All these works of Croce were published in Bari.

17. G. Fracastoro, *Il Navagero, ovvero Dialogo della Poetica,* ed. A. Gandolfo (Bari, 1947), pp. 51–53.

18. Egger, *Essai sur l'histoire de la critique chez les Grecs;* Bénard, *L'esthétique d'Aristote.*

19. D. S. Margoliouth, *The Poetics of Aristotle* (London, 1911). He defines *mimesis* as the "immaterial portrayal of the imaginary" (p. 43).

20. Aristotle, *Poetica,* ed. A. Rostagni, 2d ed. rev. (Turin, 1945).

21. Cited, n. 9 above.

22. G. F. Else, *Aristotle's Poetics: The Argument* (Cambridge, Mass., 1957).

23. Another much discussed term in the *Poetics* is *kátharsis,* the "purgation" or "purification" of emotions, produced by tragedy. However, all the fine-spun modern attempts to give a profound interpretation to this phrase (cf. Gudeman, pp. 168–71) run against the difficulty that the second part of the *Poetics,* in which Aristotle might have explained it, is missing. Some detailed observations on the effect of music on the emotions, as compared also with the effect of poetry, occur in (of all places) the *Politics* of Aristotle, 8. 5–7 (E. Barker's translation [Oxford, 1946], pp. 339–52).

8. Organic Unity in Aristotle

1. A66–67, B91–92; I. Kant, *Critique of Pure Reason,* trans. N. K. Smith (1929; reprint ed., New York, 1950), p. 104.

2. Bk. 2, ch. 2, *Wilhelm Meister's Theatrical Mission,* trans. G. A. Page, (London, 1913), p. 64.

3. Apparently rejected by Plotinus: "Beauty cannot be made to depend on magnitude" (*Ennead* 5. 8. 2).

4. For a recent general study of Aristotle in all his works, see I. Düring, *Aristotles Darstellung uns Interpretation seines Denkens* (Heidelberg, 1966).

5. Aristotle, *Metaphysics,* ed. W. D. Ross, 2 vols. (Oxford, 1924, rpt. 1958), 2: 341.

6. συνδέόμῳ "kein einheitlicher Terminus" (Gudeman, pp. 344 f.).

7. The text has "the epos from the *Iliad,*" which is interpreted as "one verse from the epic." Aristotle, *Metaphysics,* ed. and trans. J. Warrington (London, 1956), p. 39, n. 2.

8. W. Jaeger, *Aristotle,* trans. R. Robinson, 2d ed. (Oxford, 1948), pp. 74 f.

9. See the Loeb Classical Library edition of this work, ed. A. L. Peck (Cambridge, Mass., 1937), p. 28.

10. W. E. Ritter, *The Unity of the Organism, or the Organizational Conception of Life* (Boston, 1919), 1: 2–3.

11. For a full discussion of the Aristotelian meaning of Form and Matter one can still profitably consult E. Zeller, *Aristotle and the Earlier Peripatetics,* 1: 340 ff. For its bearing on the arts, cf. B. Schweitzer, "Der bildende Künstler und der Begriff der Kunstlerischen in der Antike" (1924), in *Zur Kunst der Antike: Ausgewählte Schriften* (Tübingen, 1963), 1: 11 ff., esp. 55–58. Cf. in general Whyte, ed., *Aspects of Form.*

12. Jaeger, *Aristotle,* pp. 74 f.

13. Possibly for purely stylistic reasons. *Rhetoric* 3. 3. 1606B10.

14. Aristotle explains what he means by "being prior" in *Metaphysics* Book Delta, ch. 11.

15. *Encyclopaedia of Philosophy* (New York, 1967), 3: 499.

16. G. Teichmüller, *Aristotelische Forschungen*, 2 vols. (Halle, 1867–69), 2: 68.

17. A minor difficulty remains: if Plot is the final cause of Tragedy (50A42), how can it be also its material cause? Bywater's translation of Aristotle's *Art of Poetry* meets that, p. 170, note to 50A38.

18. Cf. W. D. Ross, *Aristotle: A Complete Exposition of Works and Thought* (New York, 1909), p. 76.

19. R. A. Fogle, "Organic Form in American Criticism, 1840–1870," in F. Stovall, ed., *Development of American Literary Criticism* (Chapel Hill, N.C., 1955), p. 84. See also in the same volume H. H. Clark, "Changing Attitudes in Early American Criticism, 1800–1840," section on "The Organic," pp. 71–73.

20. F. Schiller, *On the Aesthetic Education of Man*, trans. with intro. by R. Snell (New Haven, 1954), p. 106.

21. "The Organic Concepts in Aesthetics," *Comparative Literature*, 21 (1969), p. 3. "Il concetto di unità organica in estetica," in *Critica e storia letteraria: Studi offerti a Mario Fubini*, (Padua, 1970), p. 31. "Organicism," in *Dictionary of the History of Ideas*, ed. P. P. Wiener (New York, 1973), 3: 421.

9. Later Criticism

1. Longinus, *On the Sublime*, ed. and trans. W. H. Fyfe (1927; Loeb Classical Library, Cambridge, Mass., reprint of 1946).

2. But in a recent scholarly work the attribution is renewed. The philosopher "who died in 272" is also described as "the famous critic" (A. H. Armstrong, ed., *The Cambridge History of Later Greek and Early Medieval Philosophy* [Cambridge, 1967], p. 283).

3. On the history of the term see A. O. Prickard's introduction to his translation of Longinus (1906; reprint ed., Oxford, 1954), pp. xvii–xx; J. T. Moulton's edition of Burke's *Inquiry into the Sublime and Beautiful* (London, 1958), pp. xlv ff., and S. H. Monk, *The Sublime*, 2d ed. (Ann Arbor, 1960), ch. 1.

4. On Longinus see also A. Rostagni, "Il 'sublime' nella storia dell'estetica antica" (1933), in *Scritti minori*, vol. 1, *Aesthetica* (Turin, 1955), pp. 447–518, and his edition and and translation, Anonimo, *Del sublime* (Milan, 1947), and cf. Grube, *The Greek and Roman Critics*, ch. 21. An earlier estimate is in Roberts, *Greek Rhetoric and Criticism*, pp. 122–60.

5. S. MacKenna, *Plotinus: The Ethical Treatises* (London, 1917), *Ennead* 1, p. 117.

6. Porphyry in his biography of Plotinus (ch. 4) lists this *Ennead* as the earliest, but later scholars dispute it. See F. B. De Petrella, *Il problema dell'arte e della bellezza in Plotino* (Florence, 1956), p. 166.

7. E. Panofsky, *Studies in Iconology* (1939; reprint ed., New York, 1962),

p. 133, n. 10. Panofsky had already observed this in his previously quoted *Idea*, p. 29. The translation of Plotinus cited in n. 5 above is MacKenna's, essentially if not literally "faithful," as E. O'Brien notes, *The Essential Plotinus* (New York, 1964), p. 220.

8. E. B. Osborn, *The Philosophy of Clement of Alexandria* (Cambridge, 1957), p. 17. See also his article on Clement in the *Encyclopaedia of philosophy*, 2: 122. Clement has a whole aesthetic theory, with "views parallel to Plato but not identical" (Osborn, *The Philosophy of Clement*, p. 183). He introduces also hylomorphism from Aristotle, in keeping with the Neoplatonic trend (Osborn, *The Philosophy of Clement*, pp. 181–83).

9. Proclo, *Elementi di teologia*, trans. M. Losacco (Lanciano, 1967), par. 69, p. 69.

10. Proclo, *La teologia platonica*, ed. and trans. E. Turolla (Bari, 1957), p. 89.

11. Atkins, *Literary Criticism in Antiquity*, 2: 345. Cf. Saintsbury, *History of Criticism*, 1: 118–21.

12. J. D. Boyd, *The Function of Mimesis and Its Decline* (Cambridge, Mass., 1968), pp. vii, 302–4.

13. Croce, *Estetica*, pp. 186–87.

14. *Convivio*, I, v. 13. *Le opere di Dante*, testo critico ed. M. Barbi et al. (Florence, 1921), p. 156.

15. Beare, *Greek Theories of Elementary Cognition*, p. 261.

16. Kant, *Critique of Pure Reason*, trans. Smith, "Deduction of the Categories," pp. 98–99. Cf. R. P. Wolff, *Kant's Theory of Mental Activity: A Commentary on the Transcendental Analytic of "Critique of Pure Reason"* (Cambridge, Mass., 1963).

17. See my *Benedetto Croce: Philosopher of Art and Literary Critic* (Carbondale, Ill., 1961). For Coleridge's concept of the organism, see G. McKenzie, *Organic Unity in Coleridge* (Berkeley, 1939), and my *Coleridge and German Idealism* (Carbondale, Ill., 1969), pp. 160–62.

18. Leibniz, *Opere*, vol. 2, pt. 2, p. 4, as quoted by F. H. Jacobi, *David Hume über die Glauben* (1787), in *Werke* (Leipzig, 1815), 2: 210–11.

19. "Essay on Nature," in W. Dilthey, *L'analisi dell'uomo e l'intuizione della natura dal Rinascimento al sec. XVIII*, trans. G. Sanna (Florence, 1937), 2: 182.

20. "On the Principles of Genial Criticism," *Biographia Literaria*, ed. J. Shawcross (Oxford, 1907), 2: 239, thus renovating Plato's complete formula, and giving it a Kantian tinge with the term "intuition."

21. A. Schlegel, *pace* the fanatic Coleridgians of today. Coleridge himself did not appropriate the brilliant idea of another man without acknowledgment, as was made to appear in earlier editions in which the clause about the Continental critic was unhappily omitted. See my "Coleridge and Schlegel Reconsidered," *Comparative Literature* 16 (1964): 107–11.

22. *Shakespearean Criticism*, ed. T. M. Raysor, 2d ed. (London, 1960), 1: 197.

Selected Bibliography

Aristotle. *The Basic Works.* Edited by R. McKeon. New York, 1941.

————. (pseud.). *De Mundo.* In *Sophistical Refutations.* Translated by D. J. Furley. Loeb Classical Library. Cambridge, Mass., 1955.

————. *Metaphysics.* Translated by H. G. Apostle. Bloomington, Ind., 1966.

Armstrong, A. H., ed. *The Cambridge History of Later Greek and Early Medieval Philosophy.* Cambridge, 1967.

Beare, J. I. *Greek Theories of Elementary Cognition.* Oxford, 1906.

Bosanquet, B. *History of Aesthetic.* 2d ed., 1904. Reprint. New York, 1957.

Caird, E. *Evolution of Religion.* 2d ed. Glasgow, 1894.

Caramella, S. "Unità." In *Enciclopedia filosofica.* Venice, 1937. Vol. 4, pp. 1395–1406.

Carlyle, T. *Life of Sterling. London,* 1871.

Cherniss, H. *Aristotle's Critique of Presocratic Philosophy.* Baltimore, 1935.

Coleridge, S. T. *Complete Works.* Edited by W. G. T. Shedd. 7 vols. New York, 1884.

Cornford, F. M. *Plato's Theory of Knowledge.* London, 1933.

Croce, B. *Estetica come scienza dell'espressione e Linguistica Generale: Teoria e Storia.* 1902. 9th ed. Bari, 1950.

————. *Letture di poeti e riflessioni sulla teoria e la critica della poesia.* Bari, 1959.

————. *Poeti e scrittori del pieno e del tardo Rinascimento.* 3 vols. Bari, 1945.

111

————. *Problemi di estetica*. 1910. 4th ed. Bari, 1949.

Della Valle, E. *Lezioni di poetica classica*. 2 vols. Naples, 1945–46.

De Vogel, C. J. *Greek Philosophy: A Collection of Texts*. 3 vols. Leiden, 1957–59.

Diès, A. "Le problème de l'un et du multiple avant Platon." *Revue d'histoire de la philosophie* 1 (1927): 15–22.

Emerson, R. W. *Representative Men*. 1850. Reprint. London, 1926.

Freeman, K. *The Pre-Socratic Philosophers: A Companion to Diels, "Fragmente der Vorsokratiker."* Cambridge, Mass. and Oxford, 1946.

Gadol, J. *Leon Battista Alberti: Universal Man of the Early Renaissance*. Chicago, 1969.

Gibbon, E. *Decline and Fall of the Roman Empire*. Edited by W. Smith. 8 vols. 1854. New Impression. London, 1908.

Gilbert, O. "Aristoteles Urteil über die Pythagorische Lehre," *Archiv für Geschichte der Philosophie* 22 (1890): 28–48, 145–65.

Grube, G. M. A. *The Greek and Roman Critics*. London, 1965.

Guthrie, W. K. C. *A History of Greek Philosophy*. 3 vols. Cambridge, 1967–69.

Hackforth, R. *Plato's Examination of Pleasure*. New York, 1945.

Hegel, G. W. F. *Lezioni sulla storia della filosofia*. Translated by G. Sanna and E. Codignola. Florence, 1930.

James, W. *Pragmatism*. 1907. Reprint. New York, 1956.

Kant, I. *Critique of Judgment*. Translated by J. H. Bernard. 1892. Reprint. New York, 1951.

————. *Critique of Pure Reason*. Translated by N. K. Smith. 1929. Reprint. New York, 1950.

Levin, R., ed. *The Question of Socrates*. New York, 1951.

Mazzantini, C. "Tutto." In *Enciclopedia filosofica*. Rome, 1957. Vol. 4, pp. 134–35.

Mundt, E. K. "Three Aspects of German Aesthetic Theory." *Journal of Aesthetics and Art Criticism* 17 (1959): 288–89.

Nashe, T. *Works*. Edited by R. B. McKerrow. Oxford, 1958.

Orsini, G. N. G. "The Ancient Roots of a Modern Idea." In G. S. Rousseau, ed. *Organic Form: The Life of an Idea*. London, 1972.

Padellaro, R. *Il problema cosmologico e l'antinmoia Uno-Molteplice nei Presocratici.* Pubblicazioni dell'Istituto di Filosofia della Università di Genova, N. 23. Milan, 1962.

Panofsky, E. *Idea: A Concept in Art Theory.* Translated by J. J. S. Peake. Columbia, S.C., 1968.

Pesce, D. *Idea, numero ed anima: Primi contributi a una storia del neoplatonismo nell'antichità.* Padua, 1961.

Pfeiffer, R. *History of Classical Scholarship, from the Beginnings to the End of the Hellenistic Age.* Oxford, 1969.

Phillips, D. C. "Organicism in the Late Nineteenth and Early Twentieth Centuries." *Journal of the History of Ideas* 31 (1970): 413–32.

Plato. *Dialogues.* Translated by B. Jowett. 4th ed. 4 vols. Oxford, 1953.

———. *Phaedrus.* Edited by R. Hackforth. Cambridge, 1952. Reprint New York, n.d.

———. *Phaedrus.* Edited by L. Robin. Paris, 1923.

Plato and Xenophon. *Socratic Discourses.* With introduction by A. D. Lindsay. Everyman's Library. London, 1910.

Platonis Opera. Edited by J. Burnet. 5 vols. 1900. Reprint. Oxford, 1941.

Renouvier, C. *Les Dilemmes de la metaphysique.* 2d ed. Paris, 1927.

Robin, L. *Platon: Le Banquet.* Paris, 1929.

Scholz, B. F. "A Phenomenological Interpretation of the Organic Metaphor in Literary Theory and Criticism." Ph.D. dissertation, Indiana University, 1971.

Sextus Empiricus. With an English translation by R. G. Bury. 4 vols. Loeb Classical Library. Cambridge, Mass., 1933–49.

Smith, L. P. *Unforgotten Years.* Boston, 1939.

Tatarkiewicz, W. *History of Aesthetics.* Edited by J. Harrell. 3 vols. The Hague, 1970.

Taylor, A. E. *Plato: The Man and the Work.* 1926. Reprint. New York, 1956.

Vicaire, P. *Platon, critique littéraire.* Paris, 1960.

Vlastos, G., ed. *The Philosophy of Socrates.* New York, 1971.

Wallace, W. *Prolegomena to the Study of Hegel's Philosophy and Especially of His Logic.* 2d ed. Oxford, 1894.

Whyte, L. L., ed. *Aspects of Form: A Symposium on Form in Nature and Art.* 1951. Reprint. Bloomington, Ind., 1961.

Wojcek, M. "Symbol, Organic Unity and Modern Aesthetic Subjectivism." *Zeitschrift für Anglistik und Amerikanistik* 18 (1970): 355 ff.

Wolfson, H. A. *Religious Philosophy: A Group of Essays.* New York, 1965.

Zeller, E. *La filosofia dei Greci nel suo sviluppo storico.* Translated by R. Mondolfo. Florence, 1932.

———. *Outlines of the history of Greek Philosophy.* Edited by W. Nestle. Translated by L. R. Palmer. 1931. Reprint. New York, 1955.

———. *Plato and the Older Academy.* Translated by S. F. Alleyne and A. Goodwin. London, 1876.

Index

Alberti, L. B., 5
Anaximander, 8
Anaximenes, 8
Apelles, 20
Aquinas, T., 96
Aristotle, 4, 10, 12, 24, 36, 37, 39, 41, 63–66, et passim
Armstrong, A. H., 109n2
Atkins, J. W. W., 58, 95, 110n11

Beare, J. I., 104n28
Bénard, C., 54, 75, 105n12
Bible, 91
Bignami, E., 107n2
Boeck, A., 54
Bosanquet, B., 10, 57, 101n8
Boyd, J. D., 110n12
Bundy, W. M., 107n11
Burke, E., 109n3
Butcher, S. H., 55, 92 107n10
Bywater, I., 65, 106nn3, 6, 109n17

Caird, E., 22, 103n6
Caramella, S., 101n3
Carlyle, T.: on Coleridge, 24
Chaignet, A. E., 55, 105n13
Cherniss, H., 102n16
Cicero, M. T., 96
Clark, H. H., 109n19
Clement of Alexandria, 110n8
Coleridge, S. T., 87, 95, 110nn17, 21

115

Contentualism, 14
Cooper, L., 106n8
Cornford, F. M., 9, 101n7, 103n2, 104n17, 107n14
Croce, B., 14, 21, 22, 26, 27, 87, 101n1, 103n4, 107n15, 110n17

Dante, 5, 96
D'Arcy, Father, 26
Della Valle, E., 101n1
Democritus, 20
Diès, A., 101n3
Dilthey, W., 110n19
Dobson, W., 105n1
Düring, I., 108n4

Egger, E., 54, 75, 107n9
Else, G. T., 76, 108n22
Emerson, R. W., 9
Empedocles, 20
Evenus of Paros, 38

Finsler, G., 107n2
Fish, S. E., 61
Fogle, R. A., 109n19
Fracastoro, G., 108n17
Freeman, K., 102nn12, 1
Friedländer, P., 48, 57, 105n23
Frye, Northrop, 26

Gadol, Jean, 101n3
Gentile, G., 105n8
Gibbon, E., 8
Gilbert, K. E., 59, 106n31
Gilbert, O., 13, 102n15
Glaucon, 24
Goethe, W., 23, 77
Gomperz, T., 56, 105n17
Grassi, E., 106n38
Grube, G. M. A., 59, 101n1, 104n9, 107n13, 109n4
Gudeman, A., 75, 107n12
Guthrie, W. K. C., 101n2, 102n21

Hackforth, R., 60, 103n*1*
Hall, V., 107n*15*
Hegel, G. W. F., 2, 17, 50, 102n*10*
Heraclitus, 14–18, et passim
Hesiod, 17
Homer, 14, 24
Horace, 96

Jaeger, Werner, 58, 108n*8*
James, W., 9
Joyce, J., 5

Kant, I., 3, 77, 97, 101n*1*, 108n*1*
Kantz, H. D., 106n*1*
Kermode, F., 88
Koller, M., 106n*1*
Krüger, J., 106n*38*
Kuhn, H. K., 59, 106n*31*

Lacey, A. R., 103n*15*
Leibniz, 97
Lessing, G. E., 106n*8*
Levin, R., 103n*14*
Lindsay, A. D., 103n*14*
Logos, 17
Longinus, 40, 91
Lowry, M., 5
Lucas, D. W., 106n*1*
Lucas, F. L., 107n*16*
Lysias, 32, 33, 35

McKenzie, G., 110n7
McKeon, R., 71, 107n6
Manasse, E. M., 48
Manquat, M., 106n*1*
Margoliouth, D. S., 64, 108n*19*
Marx, K., 17
Mazzantini, C., 104
Menendez y Pelayo, M., 54
Milton, J., 13

Mimesis, 66, 67–76
Monk, S. M., 109n3
Moulton, J. T., 109n3
Müller, E., 51, 105n5
Mundt, E. K., 102n18
Murray, G., 10, 64, 106n3

Nashe, T., 104n7

Oates, W. J., 61
O'Brien, E., 110n7
Organic unity, 21
Osborn, E. B., 61, 110n8

Padellaro, R., 101n3
Panofsky, E., 104n23, 106n2, 109n7
Pater, W., 88
Pesce, D., 102n9
Petrella, F. B. de, 109n6
Pfeiffer, R., 103n11
Phillips, D. C., 104n16
Philolaos, 6, 20
Philostratos, 95
Plato, 2, 3, 23, 24, 28, 30–46, 63, et passim
Plotinus, 92
Polus, 39
Polykleitos, 20
Porphyry, 109n6
Prickard, A. D., 109n3
Proclus, 110nn9, 10
Protagoras: on style, 25 39
Protogenes, 20
Pseudo-Aristotle: *De mundo*, 17
Pythagneans, 10

Raysor, T. M., 110n22
Renouvier, C., 104n26
Ritter, W. E., 108n10
Roberts, W. Rhys, 57, 109n4
Robin, L., 104n12

Ross, W. D., 108n5, 109n18
Rostagni, A., 75, 109n4

Saintsbury, G., 56, 105n16 110n11
Sandys, J. E., 57
Sappho, 40
Schiller, F., 109n20
Schleiermacher, F., 49
Schlegel, A., 110n21
Schweitzer, B., 108n11
Sextus Empiricus, 11
Sikes, E. E., 57
Smith, L. P., 102n19
Socrates, 27, 28, et passim
Solmsen, F., 106n4
Sophists, The, 23
Sörböm, G., 106n1
Spingarn, J. E., 107n15
Stefanini, L., 48, 58, 105n26, 106n28
Strachey, L., 88

Tatarkiewicz, W., 61, 102nn11, 14
Taxonomy, 21
Taylor, A. E., 59, 103n6, 104n24
Teichmüller, G., 74, 88, 109n16
Thales, 8
Theodorus, 38
Thompson, W. H., 51

Valgimigli, M., 107n9
Verdenius, W. J., 107n2
Vicaire, P., 60, 104nn10, 11
Vlastos, G., 103n14, 107n2

Wackernagel, W., 107n4
Walkley, A. B., 107n8
Wallace, W., 103n3
Walter, S., 55
Warrington, J., 108n7
Warry, J. G., 59, 106n32

Weil, R., 107n7
Weinberg, B., 107n15
Whyte, L. L., 13, 102n17, 108n11
Wilamowitz-Moellendorf, U. von, 57
Wojcek, M., 101n2
Wolff, R. P., 110n16
Wolfson, H. A., 104n25

Xenophanes, 20
Xenophon, 23, 28

Zeller, E., 13, 57, 64, 71, 102n16, 103n4, 108n11